MILLING AROUND

EXPLORING 26 MILLS IN THE MISSOURI OZARKS

BARBARA A. BAIRD

Photography by
JASON BAIRD

DEDICATION

~

This book is dedicated to my husband and soulmate, Jason Baird, who hails from the Ozarks and who is the reason I live here. He not only supported my mission by accompanying me on mill trips, but he also found time in his busy life to take and work with the beautiful photography for this book. Jason scanned all the maps and pinpointed where each mill is located. Having once been a B-52 navigator, I think this second task came easy to him. This is our first book together, which is a unique milestone for us in our 46 years of marriage. I look forward to more travels together and to taking more walks in the lovely hills and hollers of the Ozarks and beyond.

Jason Baird photographs Klepzig Mill.

One of our favorite mills, the Dillard Mill.

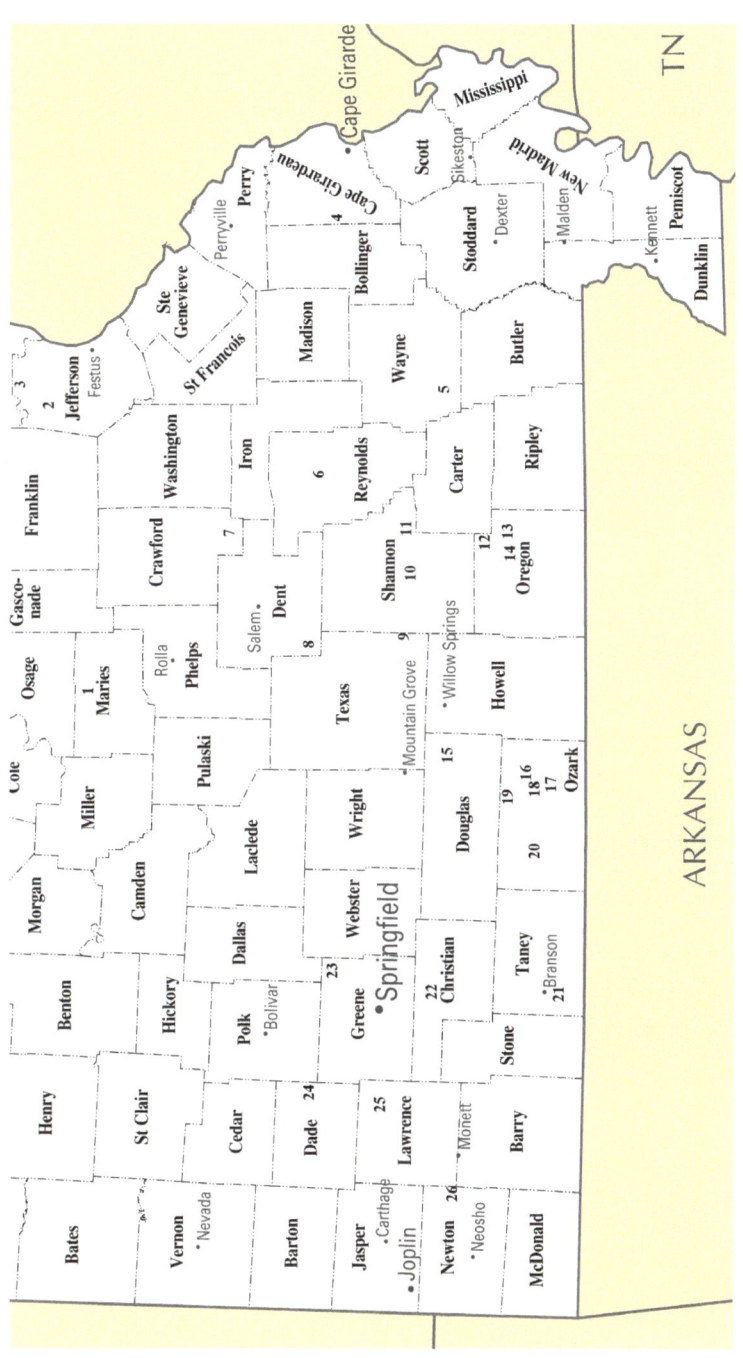

Turn the page sideways and check to see which mills are in the same counties, or which ones are near each other. The mill numbers correspond to the chapter numbers. You might be able to see a few in one day.

CONTENTS

Introduction   ix

Mill Parts   xi

1. PAY DOWN MILL   1
   Maries County

2. CEDAR HILL MILL   6
   Jefferson County

3. BYRNES MILL   10
   Jefferson County

4. BOLLINGER MILL   13
   Cape Girardeau County

5. MARKHAM SPRINGS MILL   17
   Wayne County

6. REED SPRING MILL   21
   Reynolds County

7. DILLARD MILL   25
   Crawford County

8. MONTAUK MILL   29
   Dent County

9. SUMMERSVILLE MILL   34
   Shannon County

10. ALLEY MILL   40
    Shannon County

11. KLEPZIG MILL   44
    Shannon County

12. FALLING SPRING   49
    Oregon County

13. TURNER MILL   53
    Oregon County

14. GREER MILL   57
    Oregon County

15. TOPAZ MILL   63
    Douglas County

16. HODGSON MILL   67
    Ozark County

17. DAWT MILL   71
    Ozark County

18. ZANONI MILL   75
    Ozark County

19. ROCKBRIDGE MILL   80
   Ozark County
20. HAMMOND MILL   84
   Ozark County
21. EDWARDS MILL   88
   Taney County
22. OZARK MILL   93
   Christian County
23. WOMMACK MILL   97
   Greene County
24. HULSTON MILL   104
   Dade County
25. BRITAIN MILL   109
   Dade County
26. JOLLY MILL   117
   Newton County

Resources   123
Acknowledgments   125
About the Author   127

INTRODUCTION

I am standing on the steps to Reed Spring Mill, which is on private property near Centerville, Missouri.

After my husband and I moved with our four kids to the Ozarks in the mid-1990s, we started exploring. At the time, checking out places in Missouri fell easily within our family's budget. In 2000, I became the managing editor of a small town newspaper, the *St. James Leader-Journal*. While there, I managed to convince a few other newspapers and magazines to carry my travel stories, in a column "The Accidental Ozarkian" I penned weekly for the paper.

As I searched the hills and hollers of Missouri, I met people who took me places. The first mill I visited was named Pay Down, in Maries County. In fact, it was my second column out of more than 350 throughout the seven years that I wrote it. At Pay Down, I discovered my penchant for mills, and particularly, water mills.

Between the 1830s and 1930s, hundreds of mills populated the Missouri Ozarks. Many of these mills still stand today, and a few get activated for special occasions. I've seen Joe Bob O'Neal, the miller of Topaz, open the raceway and grind corn into cornmeal. I've been onsite at the Dillard Mill, when the resident miller "let 'er rip." I can't even begin to describe the energy that pulsed throughout that old building, as the dust of the ages swirled through the air like fresh hatches on a trout stream. I will never forget those times.

We are fortunate that some people have decided to preserve these majestic tributes to industry and to a social culture of friends meeting to get a job done. It's not hard to imagine families setting up tent camps near each other as they waited for their grain to be ground into flour or meal. With beautiful streams often nearby, we can imagine a respite for swimming and fishing, and spending family time together. Many of the mills today offer museums with photographs, glimpses of days gone by.

This book features 26 mill sites still found in the Missouri Ozarks, along with their histories and present day offerings. Many thanks to Jessica Null, at the Missouri Department of Transportation, for sending the maps associated with the mills. These maps might come in handy, since you're bound to lose cell service in some of these places. Also, please use your own search engine to find out more information about each mill. I did not include web addresses in the print version of this book.

I hope you will enjoy the journeys you make to these mills, as much as the knowledge and appreciation you will gain from each visit.

~Barbara Baird, The Accidental Ozarkian

MILL PARTS

Most of the mills in this book no longer have all these parts, which once were necessary to run a mill's operations. Here is a list of common items found at a mill site. Sometimes, these pieces will be in their operating positions.

Outside a Mill

- **Mill pond** – Reservoir for a water-powered mill
- **Mill race** – A channel that diverts water from a source to the mill. Also referred to as a sluice. A headrace carries water from a source to the mill, and a tailrace conveys it away from the mill.
- **Weir** – A small dam built across a river or stream to control the water from upstream, and to control the water level. Derived from Old English *wer*, which means to "defend, dam."
- **Sluice gate** – A moveable barrier or dam that typically can be moved up and down within slots in the walls of the water channel and is adjustable by the miller, used to manage the water flow and level.

- **Flume** – Channel, controlled by a sluice gate, carrying water from the millrace to the waterwheel.
- **Waterwheel** – Typically, you'll find undershot and overshot waterwheels, which are oriented vertically so their axles are horizontal. Both types require gears to reduce the axle rotation speed to rotate the millstone, which is the ultimate goal. This gearing also increases the power delivered to the millstone. An undershot wheel, as one would expect from the name, is powered by the energy of the water flowing below the wheel. An overshot wheel requires an elevated source of water, and relies on both the power of the water flow and gravity acting on the water falling into the wheel to turn the wheel when the water hits the buckets fashioned around the wheel. It is not designed to touch a stream below. The wheels were commonly made from wood, but later, from iron and steel.
- **Turbine** – Often, you'll see old mill turbines sitting around in the mill yards. Most water mills are no longer in operation, and have been torn down. In fact, one mill sold its machinery to be melted down for World War II needs; anyway, you may see a turbine or two sitting around, or it might still be in the water near the mill. Turbines work by directing flowing water against vanes that are attached to an axle, and are more efficient at transferring power from water flow than are water wheels. Turbines began replacing waterwheels at mills sometime between 1850 and 1880. You'll see plenty of Leffel turbines, made in Springfield, Ohio, in the old mills of Missouri. The company is still in business today.
- **Headrace and tailrace** — A headrace channels water to the mill's wheel or turbine and the tailrace directs water away from the mill.

Inside a Mill

- **Buhrstone or burrstone** – sedimentary rock made of cryptocrystalline silica, originally quarried in France. The hardness and toughness of this rock made it superior for grinding grain, so many millers preferred these French buhrstones for their millstones.
- **Hopper** – Tapered wooden container that holds grain, and typically has a door in the bottom that allows the grain to flow out when the door is opened. Most milling machinery uses hoppers to control the flow of grain into the different machines; for example, millstones have hoppers mounted above them to feed grain into them.
- **Millstones** – Two large round buhrstones that grind grain. The top one (runner stone) rotates against the bottom one (bedstone), which stays stationary.
- **Furrows** – The channels you can see (sometimes only faintly remaining) that were cut into the grinding face of a millstone.
- **Gear** – A wheel on a shaft designed with teeth (or rods) that fit together with the teeth on another wheel on a different shaft, so that when one wheel turns, the other one does, and so forth. Used to transmit rotation and power from one shaft to another.
- **Belts** – Having a similar function as gears, belts are continuous straps that transmit rotation and power from rotating pulley on a shaft to another pulley on another shaft.
- **Milling machinery** – sifters, separators, etc., that convert the ground grain into the desired final products.

1

PAY DOWN MILL

MARIES COUNTY

Pay Down Mill stands forlorn, set off Highway 42 between Belle and Vienna, Missouri. The three-story grist mill, built on a foundation of limestone, is privately owned and slowly returning – from ashes to ashes – to the earth. However, it is worth a drive by, and also, it's essential that you look across the highway at the old manor house and little stone building, which has a dark history.

Back in the early part of this century, I used to run around Maries and Osage Counties collecting stories for my weekly newspaper column with a little old lady named Ethelyn Ammerman, whose father once owned the mill. She told me, "The mills and most of the property at Pay Down belonged to my family for a little over 100 years. The story goes that my great-grandfather, William Bray, brought his two sons and a daughter from England in 1856. ... My great-grandfather also brought machinery to operate a woolen mill with him. He set up his first woolen mill, and added a flour mill, at a location near Vienna, Mo. Then, he bought the Pay Down Mill in 1866. Shortly after acquiring Pay Down, the flour mill burned and he had to rebuild it in 1868."

Ethelyn Ammerman stands on the front porch of Pay Down.

She continued, "When he bought the place, the slave quarters had been standing nearly 25 years. Since my great-grandfather was from England, he had never believed in slavery and would not have owned slaves. The cut-stone slave house was built by Charles Lane, who was the first owner of the property, somewhere between 1826-1829. He had four slaves, and we know that three of them were Asa, Flora and Mingo. When my father owned Pay Down, he used the old quarters for a blacksmith shop. Several years ago, at my father's request, the county put in the new road and purposely routed the road away from the quarters. Even then, my dad appreciated history."

Ethelyn told me that Pay Down was in its heyday before and during her great-grandfather's days there. It had a post office, which was located in a back room of the flour mill and a general store.

Ethelyn continued her story: "Pay Down Mill operated because of an abundance of water, which flowed from seven springs into the main spring called Pay Down Spring. (Today, it's called Mill Creek.) Men, probably some of them slaves, dug raceways which channeled the spring water down to the mills. People have often said that Pay Down got its name from one of my ancestors, on account of his being so stingy that he insisted on having payment for goods up front. I don't think that explanation is possible, since Pay Down was here and named before my ancestors bought it.

"Here is what I've heard and what seems logical. There was a fur trader at the old general store. Someone had caught an extra-large coon and sold its skin to the trader. Later that day, another trapper slipped in the back room and stole the coonskin out. Several times that day, the same coon hide was bought and stole, bought and stole. That evening, the trader was bragging about all his coonskins, a lot for hides for so little he had to pay down. The other trappers said they wanted to see all those skins, and when the trader went to the back room to get the skins, there was only one! So, the trappers owned up to their prank and gave the trader back his money. They all had a laugh over the practical joke, and since then, the place has been called Pay Down."

In 1887, Ethelyn's grandfather, Thomas Bray – who had inherited the mill and property, built a "grand house" across the road from the mill. He purchased architectural plans for a two-story Victorian house. You can still see it. Here's how Ethelyn described it: "The house is simple, yet elegant, with a double parlor, and a beautiful hand-carved banister that curves as it goes upward. Outside, the symmetry is reproduced with two forward facing balconies. My ancestors used red trim on the front porches, and to this day, you can still see the red trim. Whenever my dad or other occupants have tried to cover the red, it always worked its way through the white paint. Four generations of my family lived in that house until my mother's death in 1970." I had the good fortune to visit the house with Ethelyn before she died.

About the slave quarters, and the slaves at Pay Down, Ethelyn said, "Sometimes, I wish I'd asked more about my family. I could have talked to Alice Johnson, a former slave, who worked for my family and the Jones' family after she was set free. She had been a slave for the first few years of her childhood and rumor has it that her father was Mr. Johnson. She knew a lot about the Bray family."

Pay Down touts a rich history, one that includes providing supplies to the Union during the Civil War and being owned (before Ethelyn's family came along) by Daniel Boone Wherry, a descendent of Daniel Boone.

Find This Mill

Pay Down is located 10 miles northeast of Vienna, Missouri, on Highway 42.

lat 38.228813° N, long 91.803278° W

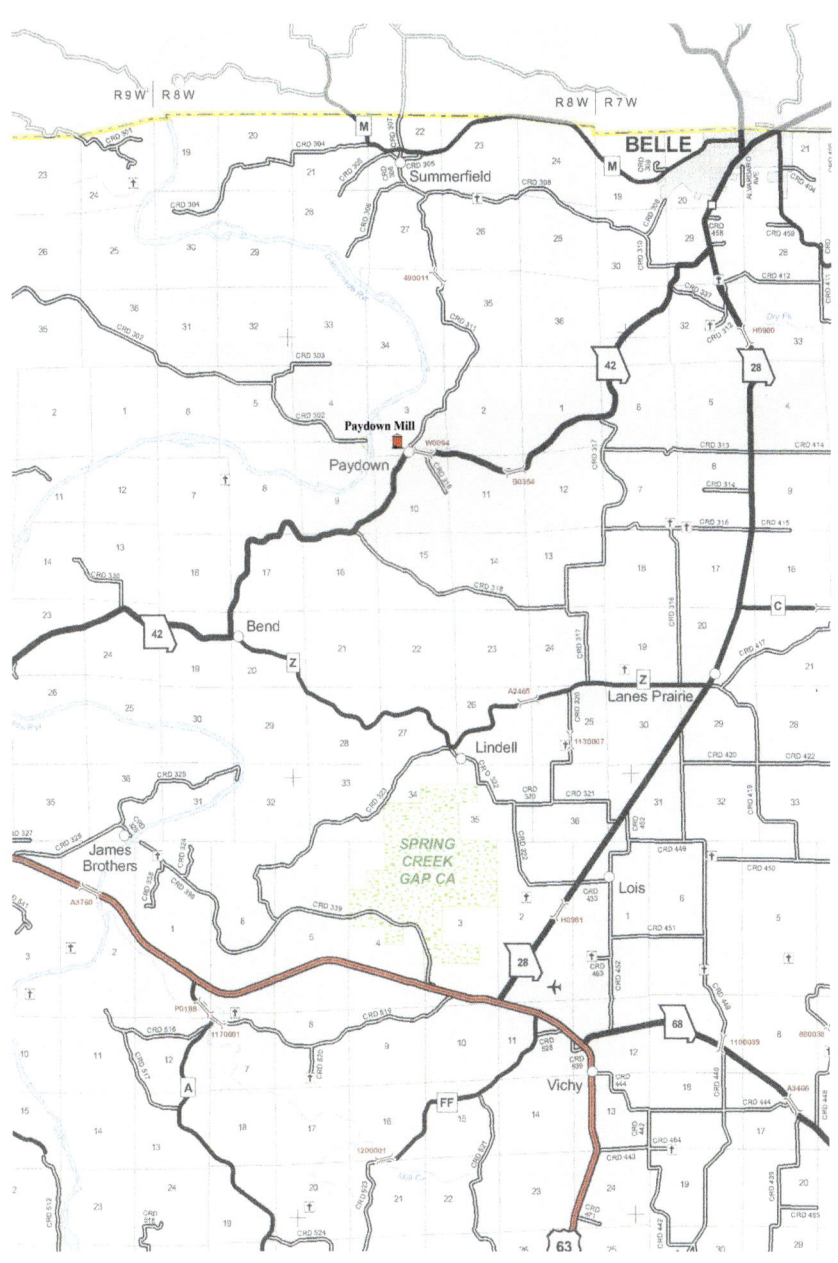

2

CEDAR HILL MILL

JEFFERSON COUNTY

I have heard that there might have been as many as 850 water mills in Missouri back in the day. Sometimes, I wonder if this number is underestimated. After all, mills ranged from private shack-type buildings that serviced a few families in a community, such as Falling Spring, to something along the lines of the big Cedar Hill Mill – regally placed on the Big River. If ever a mill was worthy of a jigsaw puzzle photo, this one claims the top prize.

The first mill recorded on this site – located in Cedar Hill, Missouri, about 30 miles southwest of St. Louis in Jefferson County, at what some might call nearly the "top" of the Ozarks region – appears around 1847 in county records. When Thomas Maddox requested the rights to build a mill on the Big River, his neighbor across the way, Conrad Beehler, objected, fearing that damming the river would flood his side. He lost in a state circuit court, and Maddox built a log and stone dam and two mills, a gristmill and a sawmill. Louis Radeacker purchased the mill and rebuilt it sometime around 1876. It's not known whether the original mill(s) succumbed to the usual – fire and/or water damage.

Radeacker built the mill that we see today in 1890, which he powered with underwater turbines. The turbines kept the mill running until 1954, when Radeacker employed a diesel engine for extra oomph. Later, the mill became completely powered by electricity.

Radeacker had seven sons, who helped him run the large operation. At first, the mill produced meal and flour. By the 1980s, at least 50 percent of the mill's products included pet food, whereas in the earlier days, it produced feed for hogs, cattle and chickens. After Radeacker's death, two of his sons, William and Albert, inherited the mill. By the 1950s, the mill had started selling ice, as well.

In 1974, Erwin Viehland purchased the business, but not the property, from two other sons who had become owners, Wilber and Walter. In 1982, James Lalumondiere purchased it and according to George Suggs, Jr.'s, book, *Water Mills of the Missouri Ozarks*, Lalumondiere had planned to use the mill to generate electricity. Note: Lalumondiere currently owns the old Byrnesville Mill, also located on the Big River, renaming it the Lalumondiere Mill and River Gardens, an event site for weddings and reunions.

While searching online, I found this site, *Mill Pictures*, and it depicts the old Cedar Hill Mill in 2004, in photos taken by Jim Miller. According to Miller, "We swam a lot in the river below the dam which my father had helped build. My Grandfather, William Fred Ficken and my dad, Oscar William Fred Ficken, told us children that the dam was made by putting large trees across the river and putting rocks over it."

You can walk out on the dam over the river and get an even closer view of the old mill. There's a city park across the river from it, with parking. We took photos from there and also, from the parking lot of the mill building. I believe the mill was listed for sale, so we felt comfortable taking a look around the outside, since it was obviously abandoned.

What to Do in the Area

On the day of our visit, a man stood on the bank fishing. You may also book a float trip from a nearby outfitter and enjoy seeing the mill from the river as you go by.

Attempts to reach Mr. Lalumondiere were not successful, through the website for his event site and by phone.

Find This Mill

From St. Louis, travel about 30 miles on US 30, turn left on CH BB, then right on Cedar Hill Road and right on Wolf Street. Parking is located near the river, across from the mill.

lat 38.350180° N lon 90.644591° W

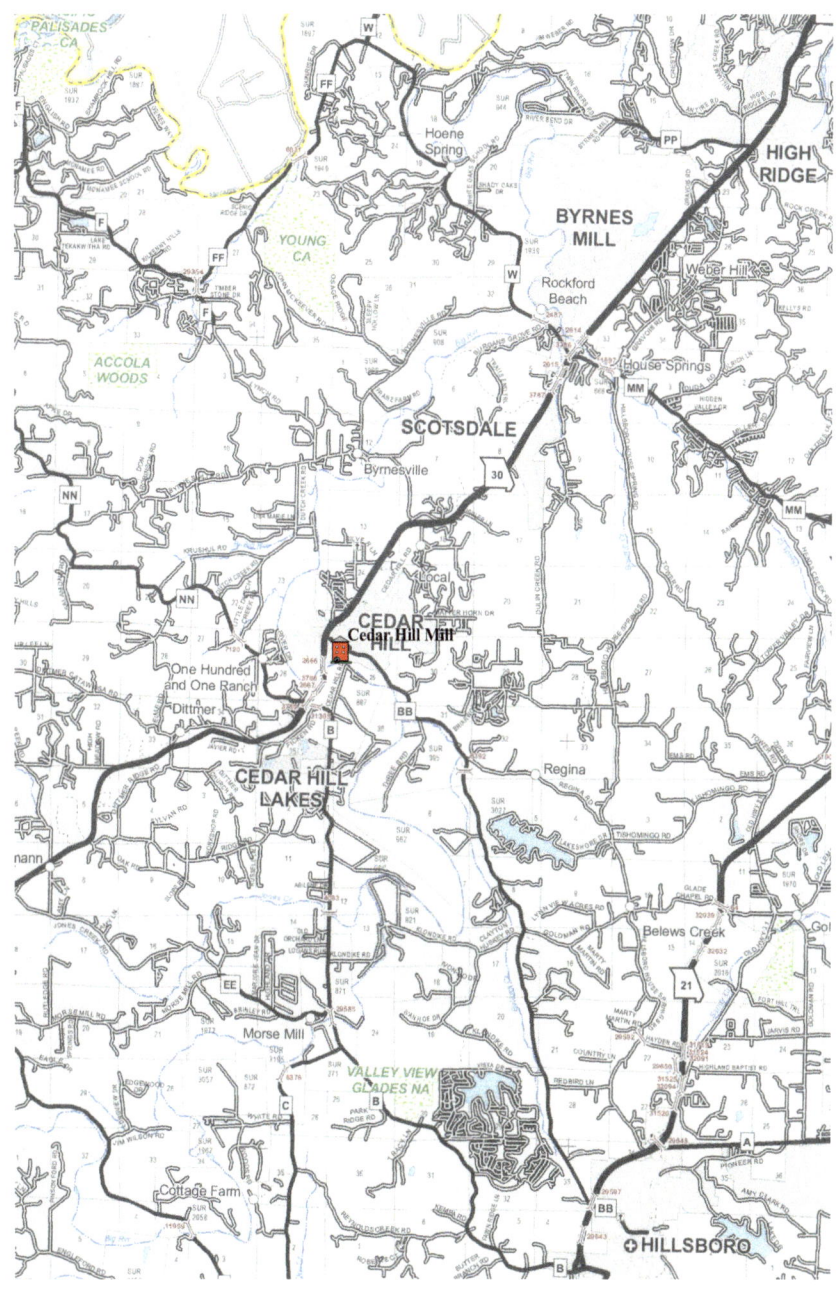

3

BYRNES MILL

JEFFERSON COUNTY

As I finished the process of visiting (and revisiting, in some cases) Missouri Ozarks' mills for this book, I found that not all mills lie intact. Sometimes, I'll see bits and pieces of what once was part of a mill, such as a weir or a dam or even, a buhrstone lying in a stream or, in the oddest case, an old overshot wheel standing upright down from where it once worked steadily. A visit to the Byrnes Mill, located in Jefferson County, afforded me the opportunity to envision this grand mill on the Big River – based on its bones.

This mill was named after Patrick C. Byrne, born in County Meath Ireland, in 1820. He and his father, James, emigrated to America in 1849, where they spent a year in Delaware before moving to St. Louis. In 1850, James bought a small farm in Jefferson County. Patrick taught one term as a schoolteacher in Meramec Township. He and his second wife, Rose, had 11 children. In 1859, Patrick and his cousin opened a store on the Big River, and six years later, he purchased a gristmill on the same river. By this time, he had purchased at least 800 acres in this area. After his death, his family opened a fishing resort near the mill area.

According to Brynes Mill, Missouri's city website, Patrick served as the city assessor, justice of the peace and also won election for associate judge of the county court (1882-1884). When he died, he left an estate worth more than $100,000.

What to Do in the Area

Byrnes Mill, the city, is named after Patrick, whose family owned the mill site and surrounding acreage until 2008. It is now a 18-acre city park. The site allows fishing, has a hiking trail along the Big River, a pavilion to rent and the historic Hagemeister House, which is a cabin from 1871 that has been relocated to this site.

The park also touts a large metal pig named Byrnie, standing inside a wooden rail pen, near a playground and restrooms.

Find This Mill

Byrnes Mill Park is located at 141 Osage Executive Circle in Byrnes Mill, Missouri. To rent the pavilion or find out more about the Byrnes Mill Park, check its website.

lat 38.437764° N lon 90.582781° W

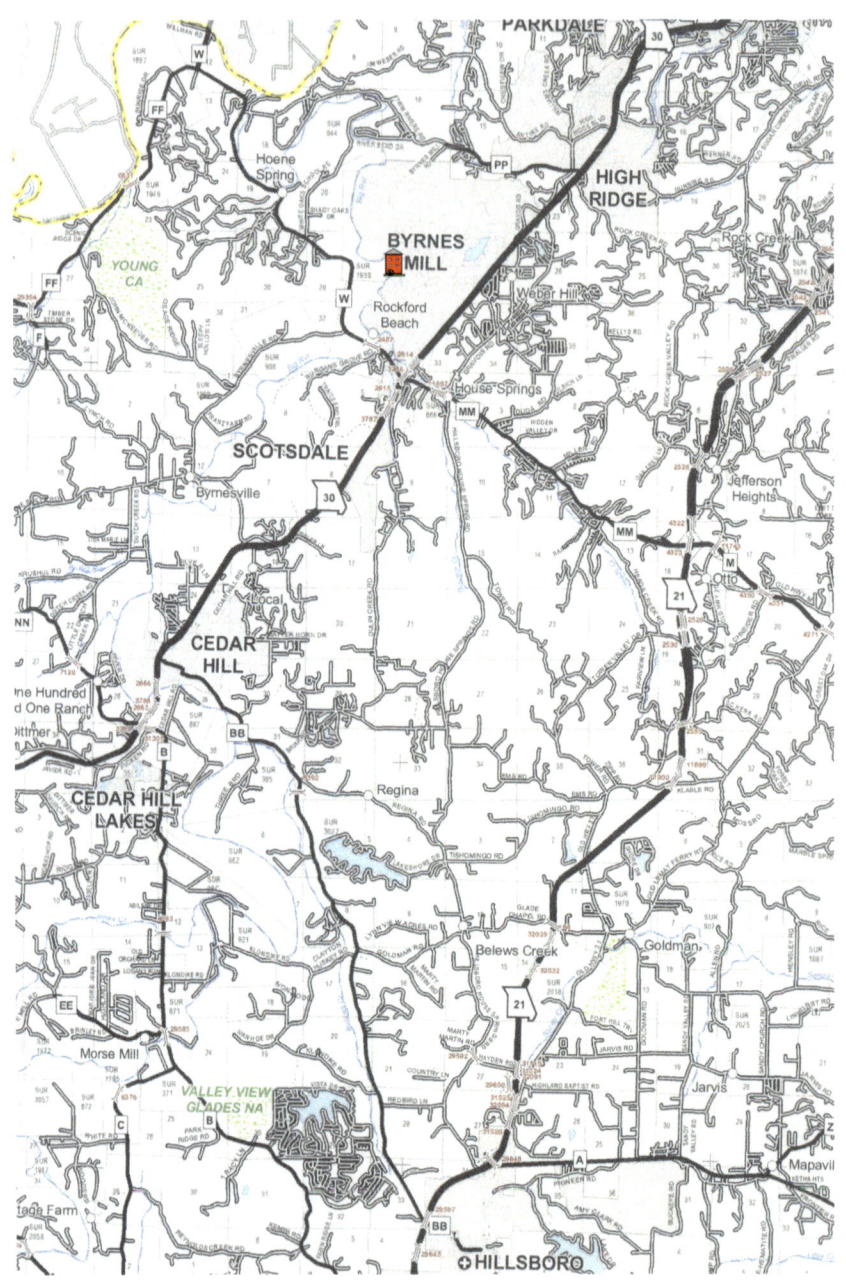

4

BOLLINGER MILL

CAPE GIRARDEAU COUNTY

I have visited a long list of mill sites in the Ozarks, and one very engaging one is Bollinger Mill in Cape Girardeau County. Having traipsed up, down and all-around in several mills, I have come to the conclusion that the main reason mills are so appealing to the general public is because they tell a story, almost soap-operatic in nature, of

bygone days. Without the history of the people who built and operated and used the mill, the site would just be another building on a
creek or river in Missouri.

Mills come with long histories — often of arson, of romance (such
as the story of the mail-order bride at Dillard Mill), of danger — or
sometimes, of man's weaknesses, such as alcohol abuse, loneliness
and selfishness. Mills served as social centers for late-19th and early
20th-century culture, and farmers brought their corn and grain,
along with their families to this mill from as far away as 100 miles. By
the 1940s, most mill operations in the country had folded due to the
penetration of rail lines and highways into the backcountry.

The Bollinger Mill touts a colorful history, too. In 1797, a North
Carolinian transplant named George Frederick Bollinger received a
land grant from Don Louis Lorimier, the Spanish commandant in
Cape Girardeau. In exchange for 640 acres, Bollinger agreed to
recruit more Carolinians to the area.

In 1800 he returned with 20 more families. Of course, it helped
that six of the men were his brothers. After recruiting workers,
Bollinger began the arduous task of building the first mill. Notice the
"first" part. Most mills are not original. Few have survived without
being burned or flooded out, and this mill is no exception.

Bollinger became successful quickly. In 1812, he was elected to be
a member of the first territorial assembly, which met in St. Louis. He
served in four sessions, until Missouri achieved statehood in 1821. It
was natural that Bollinger would become a state senator, and he was
one of the first senators to meet at the Old State Capitol in St.
Charles, Missouri. He participated in the Electoral College that
placed Andrew Jackson in the highest office in the land in 1832.

Between legislative sessions, Bollinger stayed busy improving the
mill. He replaced the lower foundation of the mill and the dam with
limestone in 1825. Teams of oxen hauled the massive blocks, which
are still there today, to the mill from a nearby quarry. When
Bollinger died, his daughter, Sarah, inherited the mill and ran it into
the ground, along with the help of her two sons. During the Civil
War, because they disapproved of Sarah's Southern sympathies and

wanted to prevent the mill from supplying grain to the Confederacy, Union troops burned the mill's top floors.

In 1866, out of necessity, Sarah sold the mill to Solomon R. Burford, who rebuilt the top structure. For this task, he chose bricks and stone. The workmen finally stopped building when they reached the fourth story. Sometime during Burford's ownership, the mill's power system changed from water wheel to turbine. The village around the mill site was named Burfordville and its post office still stands.

The mill operated until 1948. In 1953, a descendent of the Bollinger family bought the mill and gave it to the local historical society, who then gave it to the state in 1967. The Department of Natural Resources took the site, researched its history and created an impressive interpretive center within the old brick walls. Tours of the site often include the chance to see cornmeal ground between original buhrstones.

What to Do in the Area

The land around the mill has 14 picnic sites and a short hiking trail to the Burford family cemetery. Massive oak trees provide plenty of shade, and amateur photographers will delight in the possibilities for good quality photographs. There is also a covered bridge alongside the mill, one of four remaining covered bridges in the state. Bollinger Mill also has an informative website.

Find This Mill

If you want to see Bollinger Mill, travel southwest toward Cape Girardeau. The park is located off Highway 34, just outside of the city.
   lat 37.368089° N lon 89.802760° W

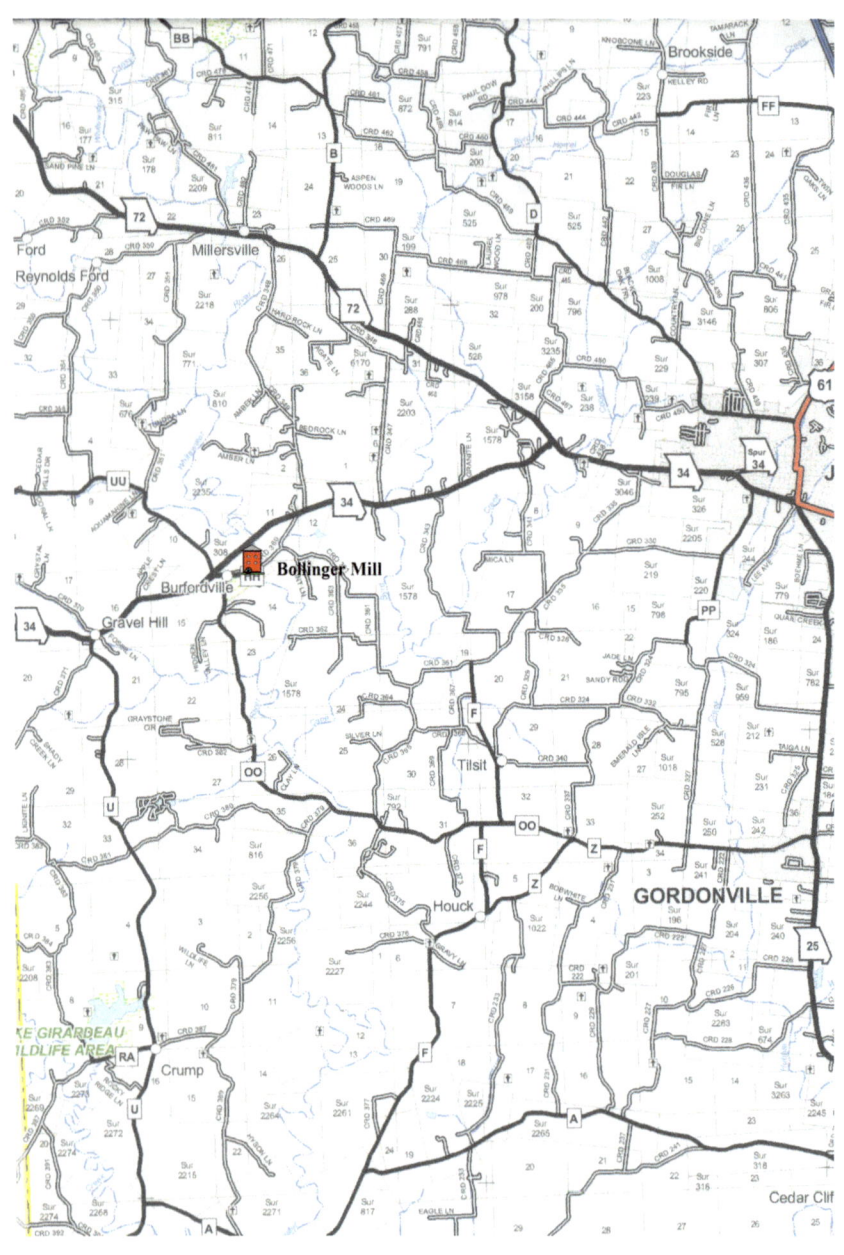

5

MARKHAM SPRINGS MILL
WAYNE COUNTY

Here's a mill site that doesn't pop up easily in searches. Thanks to a Facebook follower, I learned about Markham Springs Recreation Area and the mill, actually wheelhouse, there. This old mill site has one of the most interesting stories I've heard surrounding a mill.

The old wheelhouse sits adjacent to the Black River in the

Markham Springs Recreation Area, located within the Mark Twain National Forest near Williamsville, Missouri.

The thrill of the entire area for me, of course, is the old mill site itself. As many mill sites go, there was once a gristmill with an undershot wheel onsite here, too – well before 1850. According to a website article about "Markham Springs History," the site also held a sash sawmill that cut more than 1,500 board feet of lumber daily. This is not unusual, and in our travels, we have seen mill sites function for more than one purpose.

Sometime in the later 1800s, Bill and Jo DeHaven constructed a large, two-story gristmill with a 14-foot overshot wheel here. It boasted new machinery required for a proper flour mill.

The mill acquired its present name from owner Jefferson Markham, who purchased the property in 1901, and ran it as a gristmill until 1907. The mill went unused until the 1930s, when Rudolph Fuchs purchased it and replaced the old mill with the present-day wheelhouse.

Near the mill sits the Fuchs House, which is a beautiful five-bedroom stone and concrete house, built by Fuchs in the late 1930s. Fuchs constructed the present-day wheelhouse, at the site of the old mill, to produce electricity. He never used the waterwheel to generate power, because Rural Electrification Administration arrived on the scene, and offered a much better solution.

He also built a dam on a spring near the mill. There's an enormous mill pond in front of the house. The pond receives almost five million gallons of water a day from six springs that feed into it.

The US Forest Service (USFS) acquired this site in 1965. Several years later, in 2010, local craftsmen renovated the house, under permit from the Mark Twain National Forest. In return for their services, the craftsmen and their families get to use the location during the year on the dates of their choices, and then, it is available for rental during certain times of the year.

You can see that at one time, the USFS opened the wheel house for visitors, and there are old displays standing inside the room. The little building is no longer open for visits.

On the day we visited, we were the only people onsite. We could explore all around the old mill site, and enjoyed the view with wild flowers and a rustic old overshot wheel. This would be a fine place to stop for a picnic.

What to Do in the Area

The area offers hiking trails, such as the Eagle Bluff trail, whereas the name would indicate – you can see birds galore.

It also offers primitive camping sites, as well as a campground with single and double sites for tent and RV camping, with electric hookups. It also has river access for boating, fishing and canoes.

Find This Mill

From Poplar Bluff, take Highway 67 north for 14 miles, then drive west on Highway 49 for 9 miles (about 3 miles past the town of Williamsville). Take the first right after crossing the Black River to enter Markham Springs Recreation Area.

lat 36.978138° N lon 90.602536° W

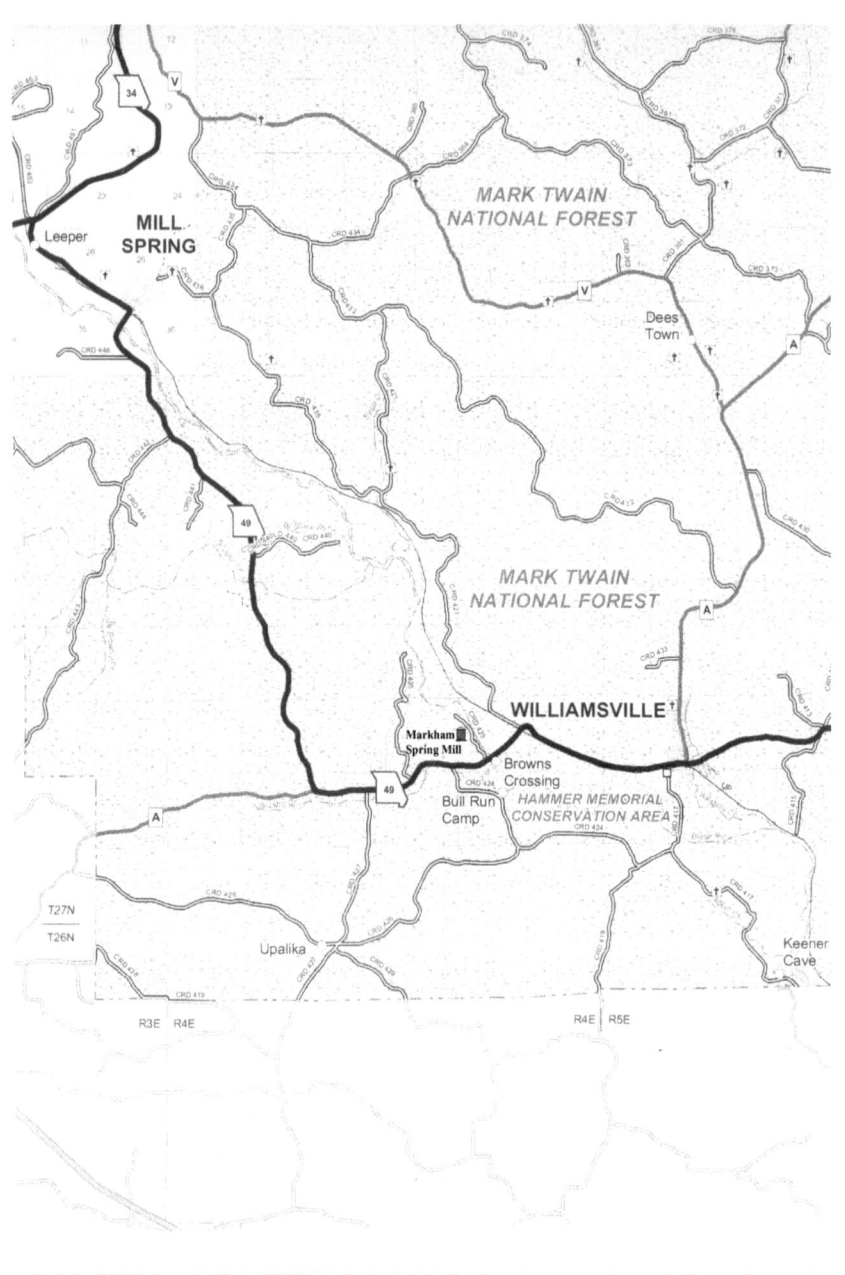

6

REED SPRING MILL
REYNOLDS COUNTY

Reed Spring Mill is not to be associated with the small town of Reeds Spring, Missouri. In fact, they are about 212 miles apart. Reeds Spring is located slightly southwest of Springfield, and Reed Spring is in Centerville, Missouri, in Reynolds County.

To have a mill and a spring within a city's limits is unusual in itself. But that's not all that is different about this setting. It sits on private property, and the owners graciously allow people to meander about the setting. They not only allow folks to hike up to the beautiful blue gushing spring, but also, to go inside the old mill building.

History of Reed Spring Mill

I have seen the name written as Reed Spring and Reed Springs. In actuality, it could be Reed Springs (just as Alley Spring is often referred to as Alley Springs and Bennett Spring as Bennett Springs). It seems there is always more than one output at any spring; so technically, there is more than one "spring."

Reed Spring appears from the side of a hill and forms a beautiful blue pond, and then meanders, flows and grows toward the Black River. The spring lies behind the mill.

It's easy to see why Nathaniel Scott built the first mill onsite here in 1881, grinding corn and flour. He then added a sawmill to provide lumber so that settlers could build homes and businesses in the town around the mill. By 1915, history records that someone named Dr. Shy decided to use the power from the water at this source to generate electricity. That meant the overshot wheel had to go, and he had a turbine installed to produce more power.

About the electricity, *Missouri Vacation!* wrote, "Though the lights were bright at the mill, but dim in town, this supplied the town's electric until 1929. The original building and wheel were taken apart, board by board, and sent to San Francisco for exhibition at the 1939 World's Fair. This display is now in storage at the Smithsonian Institution in Washington, D.C."

A replica of the original mill was built at the site in 1973, complete with an overshot wheel. Step inside the small building, and you can see the water running hard underneath.

On the late winter day that we visited the setting, the water gushed down the hillside and under the mill. The spring pond reflected a brilliant blue.

What to Do in the Area

The town lay quiet, and we enjoyed seeing the Reynolds County courthouse, built in 1871. Here is where 100 Union soldiers camped in 1863, before they were captured by Confederate Rev. Jesse Pratt.

Find This Mill

To find the mill, travel to Centerville on Highway 21, and go west on Pine Street for ½ mile. Please be cognizant that this setting is private. Today, the owners of the mill keep the setting groomed as if it were a park. There's even a picnic table onsite.

lat 37.433845° N lon 90.949187° W

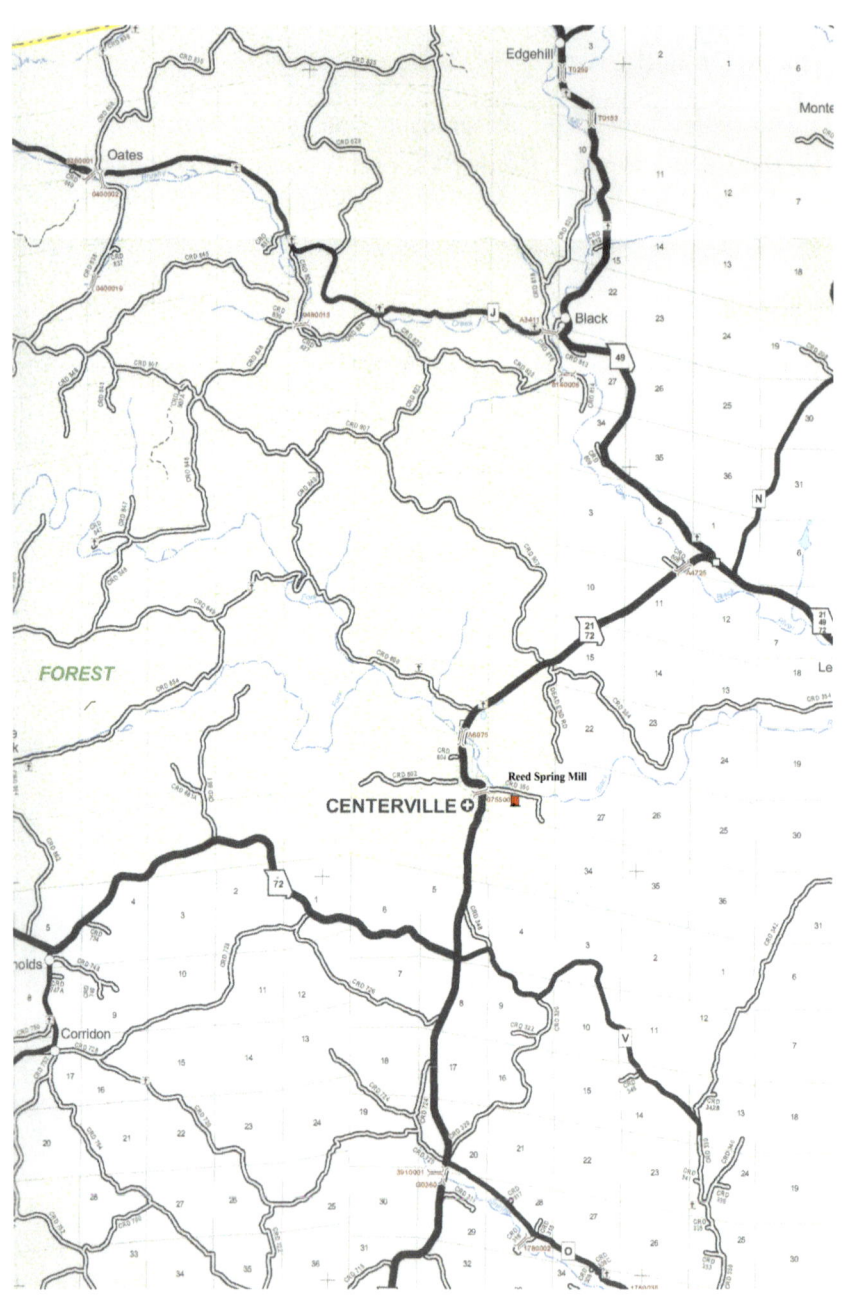

7

DILLARD MILL
CRAWFORD COUNTY

The two-story, cherry red Dillard Mill sits overlooking the junction of the Huzzah and Indian Creeks in Crawford County. Alongside the mill, a waterfall spills into a huge reflecting pound. The overall site appears idyllic and well deserving of the title, "the mill on the hill."

The history of Dillard Mill rivals its colorful exterior, because it speaks of adventure, romance and a disaster. The first mill on the site,

Wisdom's Mill, was built in the 1850s and soon became home to a small community named Dillard, after Joseph Dillard Cottrell. In 1887, a post office was established and 10 years later, the mill burned down.

In 1900, two Polish immigrants, a brother-sister duo named Emil and Mary Mischke, bought the property. They immediately built a new mill, using some of the salvaged timbers from Wisdom's Mill. The Mischkes then brought the mill up to current technological standards by installing steel roller mills instead of buhrstones for grinding. They also installed a turbine, and the mill opened for business again in 1908.

By 1917, the mill attracted farmers with their grain, and also touted a general store.

After Mary sold her portion to Emil, he ran the business for another 10 years. He must have been lonely, because at the age of 66, he did what a bachelor out in the sticks might do to find a wife – he paid for a mail-order bride from California.

The new Mrs. Mischke, however, was not enthralled with the Ozarks and the gristmill. After a few years, she convinced her husband to take her back to California.

In 1930, Emil sold the mill to another entrepreneur, Lester E. Klemme. He continued milling flour and livestock feed. He also built cabins on the site and opened a resort called Old Mill Lodge. For a few dollars, a person could swim or fish in the pond, stay overnight in a cabin and eat with Klemme in his home.

By 1957, across the nation gristmills declined operating. Klemme shut down the milling side of his business, but kept the resort open until the 1960s.

In 1974, Klemme sold the mill to the not-for-profit L-A-D Foundation. In 1975, the Foundation leased the mill, plus 132 acres to the Missouri Department of Natural Resources. It is listed as a state historic site.

The machinery has not changed since it was last used in the 1950s, although on a recent trip we were told about a repair to one of the milling machines. The old machines, built in St. Louis, feature trap doors, elaborate metal catches, fancy knobs and hand-carved wooden paddles.

I first visited the mill back in 2000. Not much, if anything, has changed in 22 years. After walking through the mill that I hadn't visited for more than 20 years, I could hardly wait to see it in action again. This is a rare thing, to be able to experience this – talk about a trip down Memory Lane. The old building came alive, with pumping and whirring and banging. I think I saw the dust of the ages dancing in the air.

While this occurred, more than 2000 gallons of water per minute gushed through the turbine.

What to Do in the Area

Tours are available, and the site offers fishing, Mill View Trail and picnic tables. For more information, visit the Dillard Mill State Historic Site website.

Find This Mill

If you would like to visit Dillard Mill, follow Highway 19 to Cherryville and then take 49 to Dillard. Look for the signs.

lat 37.717849° N lon 91.206504° W

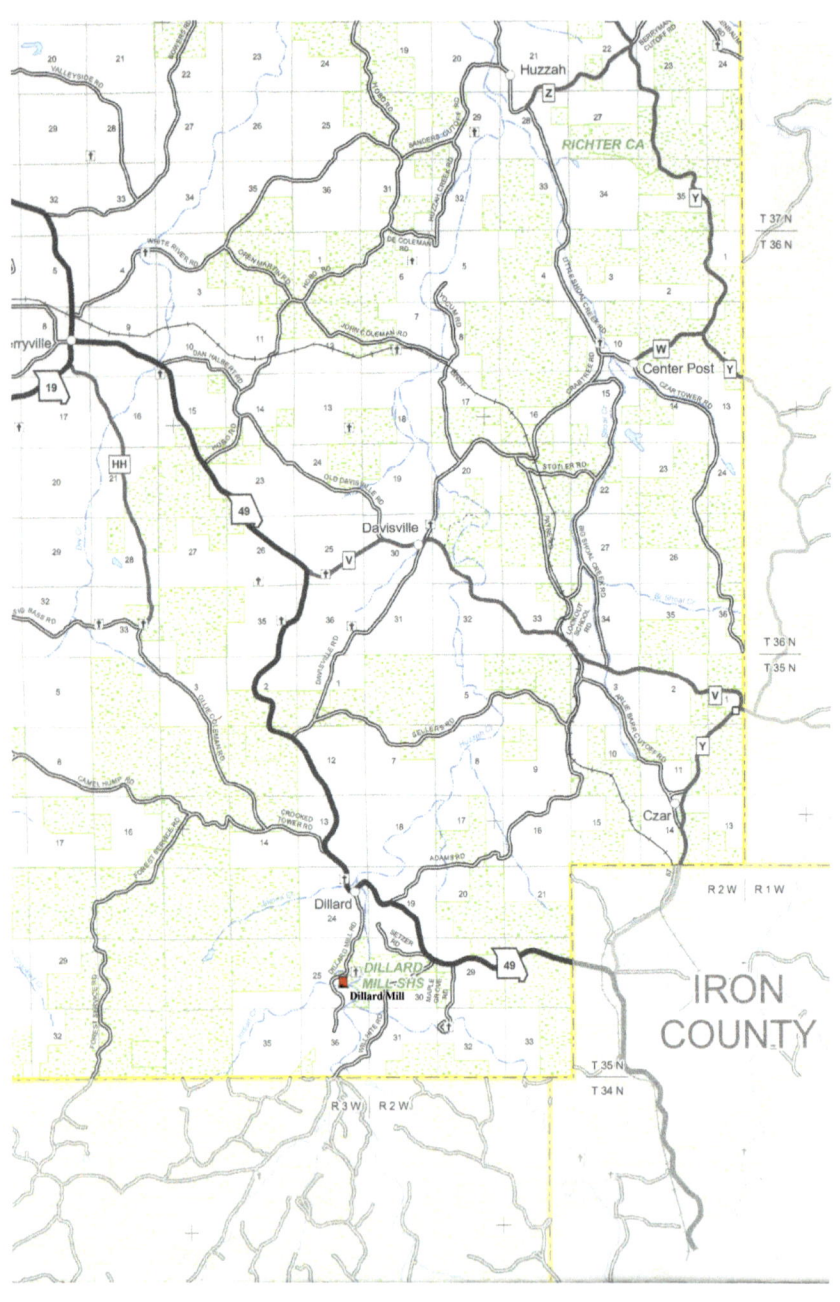

8

MONTAUK MILL
DENT COUNTY

Montauk State Park, located near Salem, Missouri, is one of the most popular vacation spots in the state, largely in part because of its popular trout stream (Current River) and fish hatchery on-site. The park also holds other treasures – namely historical Civilian Conservation Corps (CCC) structures, along with its huge gristmill. Plus, visitors may camp, hike, bike, stay in a lodge or cabins on-site and generally enjoy the great outdoors in this pristine setting.

Park naturalist Kristie Nelson manages the natural and historical resources at Montauk, including offering nature programs and tours of the historic gristmill. Though she is a relative newcomer to Missouri and Montauk, she feels at home in this rural setting.

Kristie said about 600,000 people per year visit the park. She added, "It's a specific destination, at the end of the road. People are coming here for the purpose of visiting the park. By far and away, fishing is the biggest draw. Montauk is one of Missouri's trout parks, and there's a hatchery and nightly stocking here, so fishing is really good."

When asked about the mill, she said, "The mill has such a commanding draw to it. It's like the heart of the park – centrally located, big, mysterious. It just oozes a history and a story to tell, so I think it draws the attention of anyone who comes here."

History of Montauk Mill

Kristie described the history of Montauk, which once had two mills operating in the valley. She said, "The very first mill was built around 1835, not long after the valley was permanently settled by white settlers around 1829. The original mill was known as the Holloman Mill. It was on the same parcel that our current mill is, but about 100- to 200-yards downstream and closer to the river. The second mill was built around 1860, and known as the Stevenson's Mill. That was located closer to the main spring, closer to where the fish hatchery and old stone CCC footbridge is today. That mill operated for some time, and the Stevensons were involved in the community. In 1881, a woman named Elizabeth Hickman purchased the Holloman Mill and her son, Timothy, operated it and did some repairs on it. In 1894, they tore that one down and rebuilt a new mill in the approximate location of the mill we have today. Yet as soon as that third mill was completed, it burned down – suspected of arson. Timothy immediately rebuilt with a famous millwright named William Furry, and this is the mill we have today."

The mill was a gristmill, and ground flour and corn on-site. "The corn grinding was simpler than flour milling because it didn't involve the sifting and some other processes required." When asked if the equipment is functional, she was doubtful. "From what I hear, they got the corn grinder going by way of a tractor in the 1990s. Unfortunately, any future operations are unlikely."

She added the hydropower aspect from the river is a "thing of the past." However, she pointed out the fact that the waterfall – or mill dam – is still on-site and in the same location as when the mill was in its heyday. She said, "It's still used, and it's been built upon and refurbished, but it's still the old original mill dam. But today, it's shunting water to feed the fish rearing pools, right below the mill."

Kristie said most of the machinery in the mill is original, except for the corn grinder display and the three steel roller mills. The roller mills went to support WWII steel production efforts in the 1940s. Luckily, replacements like the originals were acquired for the Montauk Mill by the state park system.

As for the mill's buhrstones, she said the original ones lie in the front of the mill because the CCC removed them to preserve the floor and lessen the weight overall in the building, back in the 1930s. The mill continued to operate through 1927.

Kristie also mentioned an interesting location for an old buhrstone: "There is a buhrstone over by the campground, right below the bridge on the downstream side in the river. It's either from one of the mills that got torn down or was simply a worn out stone that was replaced. That's just a guess!"

Hauntings and Disasters?

Regarding hauntings or disasters often associated with mills, she remarked, "I've heard a lot of the legends here, but I've not heard anything too ghostly about the mill. One of the millers did have ill health, which may well have been related to the white lung, and he was heartbroken when he had to sell because it gave his life a lot of meaning and purpose. There certainly have been Civil War-related hangings and deaths in the park ... but nothing that I know of associated with the mill."

Renovations at Montauk Mill

Kristie mentioned renovations are in the works at the mill. "Being an old building, things wear out. We are planning to reroof the entire structure; it's probably some years out for the whole building. But, for this year, we're replacing the roofing (corrugated metal) on the south side of the building, which is where the majority of the leaks are ... so that will clear up most of our problems. This year, too (2023), we're going to reassess and repair the board and batten on the entire structure. Whenever possible, we reuse the old wood, and our process of fixing old historic buildings is precise and goes through review, with an eye toward maintaining as much authenticity as possible. Then we'll refinish the whole structure with a wood-preserving finish, because it looks a little threadbare."

Kristie said, "Once fishing season starts, we will open for tours throughout the week. On Sat., May 13, we're bringing back our Mill Days celebration, where we bring in crafters and historic demonstrators. Since you asked about ghosts, in late October we have a spooky event, where it's a reenactment and host a 'Haunting of the Mill' event, where spirits of the past appear to tell their stories."

Visit Montauk State Park online.

Find This Mill

Montauk Mill is located on MO-199 S in the southeast corner of Dent County. It lies to the east of Highway 63, near Jadwin, Missouri.

lat 37.450411° N lon 91.684203° W

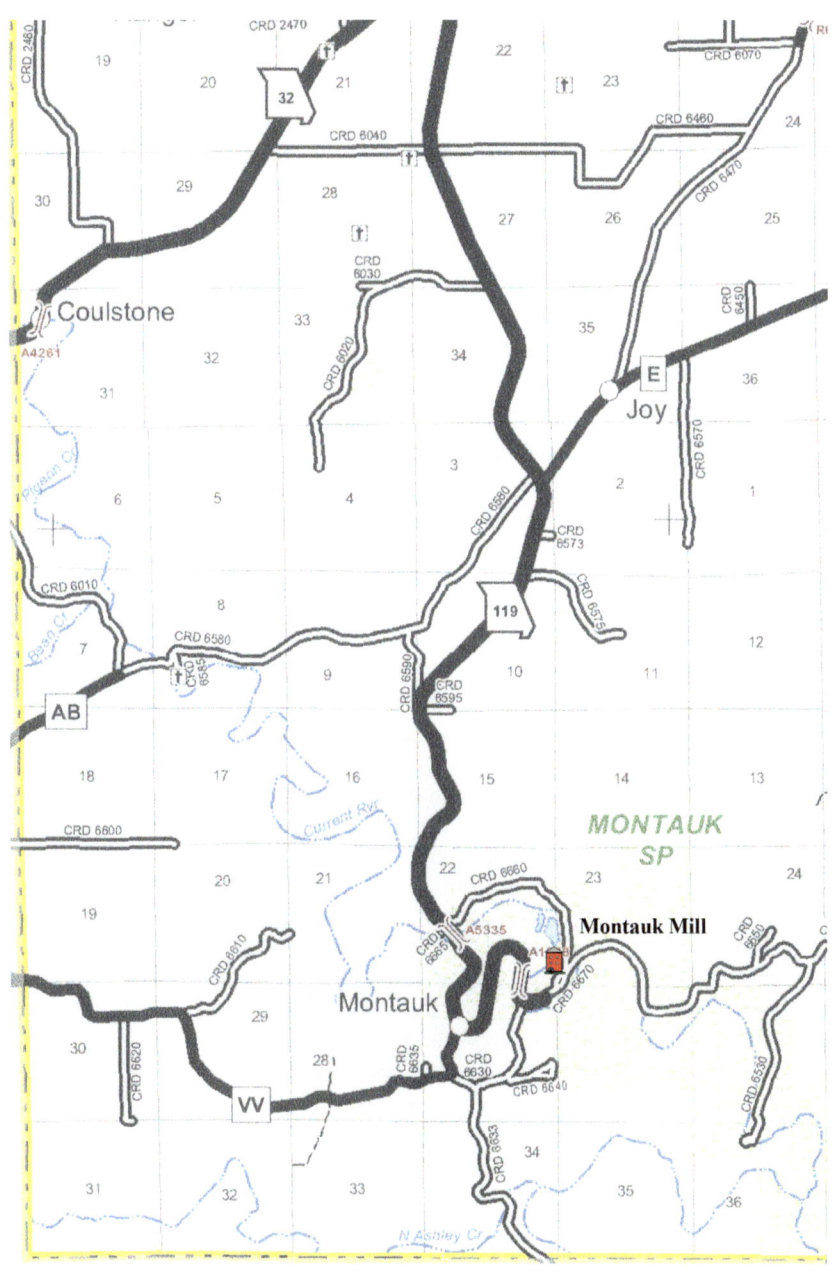

9

SUMMERSVILLE MILL
SHANNON COUNTY

My trip to the Summersville Mill was after I nearly completed my list of mills for this book on what began as water mills of the Missouri Ozarks; and then, after seeing Summersville, I decided to add it and another steam-powered mill to the lineup (Wommack, in Fair Grove). Although this mill never received power from a stream into a race-way, it did use a mill pond fed by springs that served as the water source for steam power, which was later replaced by two kerosene powered hit-and-miss engines. Its history bears a mention in this book, and its beautifully preserved interior also deserves a chapter.

After my husband (who is the book photographer) and I toured the mill, courtesy of Summersville resident Charlotte Siedsma, we talked about how throughout this mission of visiting mills, we have met people who truly have a passion for keeping history alive. Charlotte, throughout the years, and her husband, Richard, have been instrumental, along with many members of the Summersville community and the West Plains tourism agency, for keeping the interest in this mill going.

History of the Summersville Mill

Today's building dates earlier than 1886. Jim McCaskill already ran a post office and general store on the square, in Summersville, and added some milling equipment. A few years later, he expanded the operation and sold the original equipment to Horace Greeley, who then sold it to McCaskill's brother, George Washington McCaskill, over at Alley Spring for use in the mill located there. You can still see that equipment at Alley today. As a result of the expansion and new equipment, the mill (in its heyday) could produce 60 barrels of flour and grind 100 bushels of corn per day.

As was the usual for Missouri Ozark mills, the Summersville Mill changed hands throughout the years, and eventually sold to the Joe Donovan family in 1927. The mill operated until 1972, and by that time, it mainly ground feed for animals rather than for human consumption.

The Donovans sold the mill to Ronnie Reeves, then in 2002, the Reeves donated the mill to the Revitalization and Action Board of Summersville, in 2002. By 2007, work had began to restore it. Charlotte said, "Clean up started in 2007, and as the years went, we added new siding. One of the gentlemen that is a forester cut the logs on his property and we took it down to Smith Flooring in Mtn. View and had it milled. We brought it up to the pallet factory here and they dried it and sliced it into boards. The Amish put it up. The roof was given to us by White Industries over in Willow Springs."

She pointed to the scale, and said, "The scale is as accurate as the day it was [installed] here. It's a Fairbanks scale, and I've called Fairbanks several times, and they say. 'Yeah, we'll get back to you,' and I'm still waiting."

Charlotte showed us how a miller would use the scale, adjusting various weights. "Depending on the weather, it will vary, but it will be within ounces." Charlotte said they had the children from a visiting kindergarten class stand on the scale: "It was an absolute riot and they weighed over a ton."

Local people donated flour sacks from the mill, and these are on display in a glass case. Charlotte, who is from northern Illinois, said she and her sister wore flour sack dresses during their younger years.

The tour continued upstairs, and we peered inside a storage bin area as Charlotte continued to explain the milling process. This mill ground flour, corn and later oats. The mill has all its original machinery, and Charlotte says it all works, because they've tested it. Throughout the mill, you can see the handiwork of the milling machinery, down to the elegant craftsmanship and detail in hardware. The dedicated milling equipment came from Moline, Illinois. Some of the other equipment, such as the flour bag filler, came from Richmond, Indiana.

Charlotte showed us an interesting piece of equipment – a horsehair brush attached to a wooden block sized to fit within a grain chute – that a miller would attach to the belt within the chute so the brush block would circulate and clean out things such as hornets' nests, spider webs, etc. She also showed us a new wooden auger in storage that they may be willing to sell or trade in the future to another mill.

Charlotte Siedsma and Denise Bullock met after our tour, because Denise stopped by on her way home to Indiana. Denise's great-grandfather, William Jackson (Jack) McCaskill, owned and operated several mills in Missouri, including the Summersville Mill.

What to Do in the Area

This might be the time to see some of Missouri's famous springs, such as Blue and Round. Or, go to visit Alley Spring, which is only 14 miles away from Summersville.

Find This Mill

The Summersville Mill is located just east of the Summersville square, on the corner of Elm Avenue and Route 106.To learn more about the Summersville Mill, or to set up a tour, email, tourism@ westplains.gov.

lat 37.179264° N, lon 91.653775° W

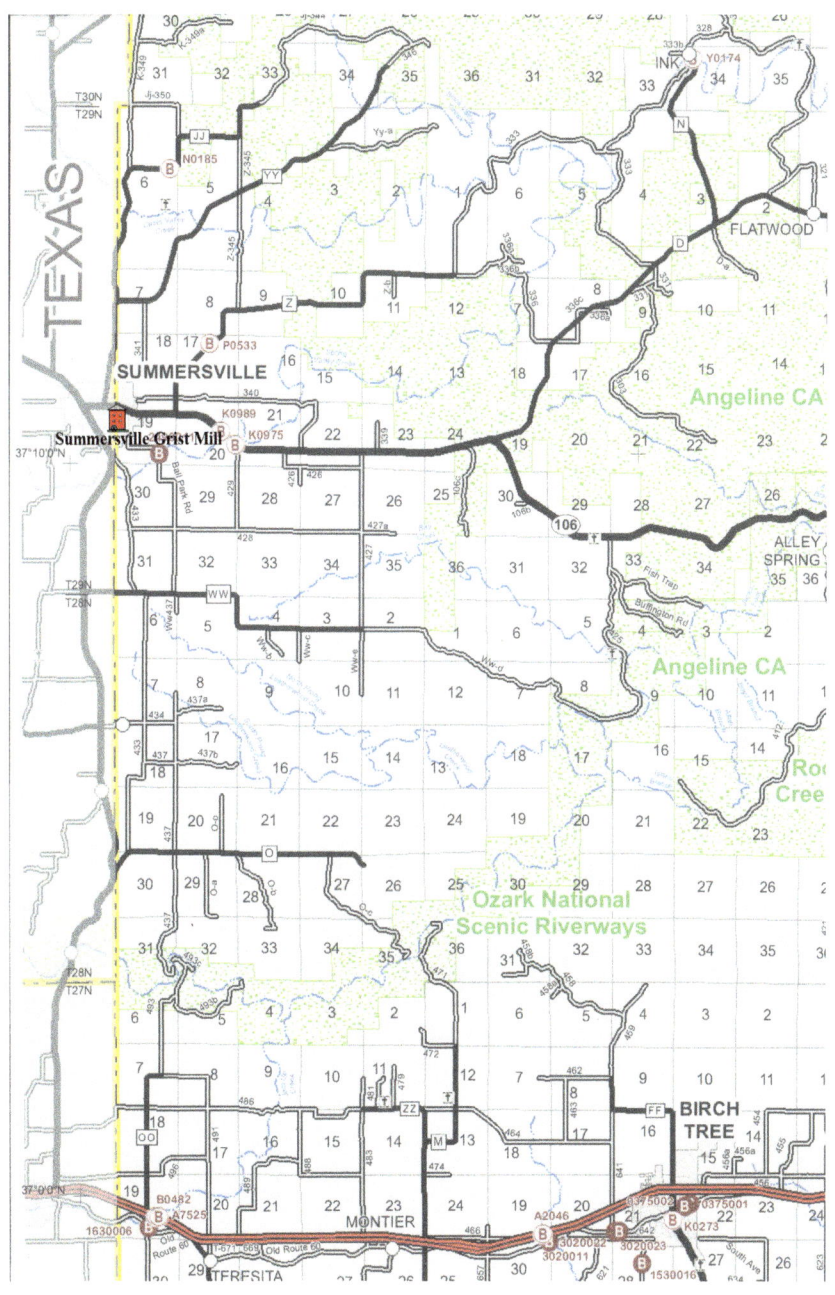

10

ALLEY MILL
SHANNON COUNTY

It's the most photographed mill in Missouri. It's a place you'll want to take visitors to while they're in the Ozarks, and is a part of the treasure trove called the Ozark National Scenic Riverways. If you have never been to the this mill, it might be the time to go. The mill stands on a dramatic natural site where the seventh largest spring in the state gushes forth.

Alley Spring comes from a conduit that reaches at least 3,000 feet underground. Rain and water runoff from nearby Summersville (14 miles to the northwest) snakes its way through dolomite cave passages. The spring powered the iconic mill back in the day; the tailrace eventually makes its way to the Jacks Fork River. The spring is still flowing strong today, and contributes an average 81 million gallons of water daily to the Jacks Fork – fueling many Ozarks canoe outfitter businesses.

Built by George Washington McCaskill in 1894, it served as a merchant mill and claimed high tech equipment such as roller mills and turbine power, as opposed to grist mills and water wheel power. Today's Alley Mill replaced a mill that had been onsite since 1868. At first, it touted white paint with green trim, but at some time, someone decided to paint it cherry red.

This site also had a post office, named Alley, after a family that settled here. As with most milling sites, it saw lots of life and recreation, as farmers and their families brought grain to be ground into flour. History records dances, roller skating and baseball games as ways to pass time while the grain processing occurred.

Now operated by the U.S. National Park Service, the mill has three floors and a basement. Visitors may not go into the basement, and this was the powerhouse of the former mill in all its glory, where elevators and conveyor belts whirred and snapped. On the first floor, operators dumped corn and wheat into bins and raised the harvest to chutes that sent the grain to milling machines. These machines ground the grain and sent it to yet another machine, where it was ground again, eventually ready for baking as flour.

On the second floor, more sifting occurred. First, the mill used a silk screen bolter, which had a silk covered drum that spun in the middle of the machine. Flour entered the drum, then got forced out through the silk. You can see a horsehair brush on the machine that brushed flour off the silk. An auger then moved the flour into an exit chute. Later, a swing sifter replaced this technology. It used cloth-covered wire mesh screen that sifted the flour into chutes below.

Up in the attic (third floor), which also is not open to the public, stood belts that operated all the second floor processes.

Outside, if you look under the back porch, you'll see the turbine pit, which houses a 35-inch Leffel turbine. This turbine brought the power into the basement to begin the milling process, and a miller could control the speed of the turbine, which in turn, controlled the amount of water that entered.

What to Do in the Area

You can easily spot Story's Creek School, a one-room schoolhouse from the early 1900s, moved here from another location. It also served as the neighborhood church. It is open from Memorial Day weekend through Labor Day weekend. It represents, according to the National Park Service, a rule that schoolhouses – unless made of logs – needed to be white on the exterior. (Supposedly, the interiors were supposed to be painted light blue.) We stepped inside and back in time, where the wooden desks that seated two students, sat in straight rows and held small chalkboards.

Up a hill from the schoolhouse, stands the general store, where you can purchase postcards, souvenir items, books, treats and sarsaparillas out of the cooler. Or, you can sit and rock on the front porch for a spell.

The site contains 795 acres, with trails that begin near the old mill. Picnic sites have been created near the spring branch, and there are two large pavilions within walking distance of the Jacks Fork River.

If you like to golf, you may enjoy the combination called the Roy L. Beck Municipal Golf course and Walking Trail, a 9-hole par, 36-layout golf course with a two-mile nature trail that begins on the bank of the Jacks Fork River and culminates on a ridge top.

Find This Mill

Alley Spring Mill is located six miles west of Eminence on State Route 106.

lat 37.154215° N lon 91.442011° W

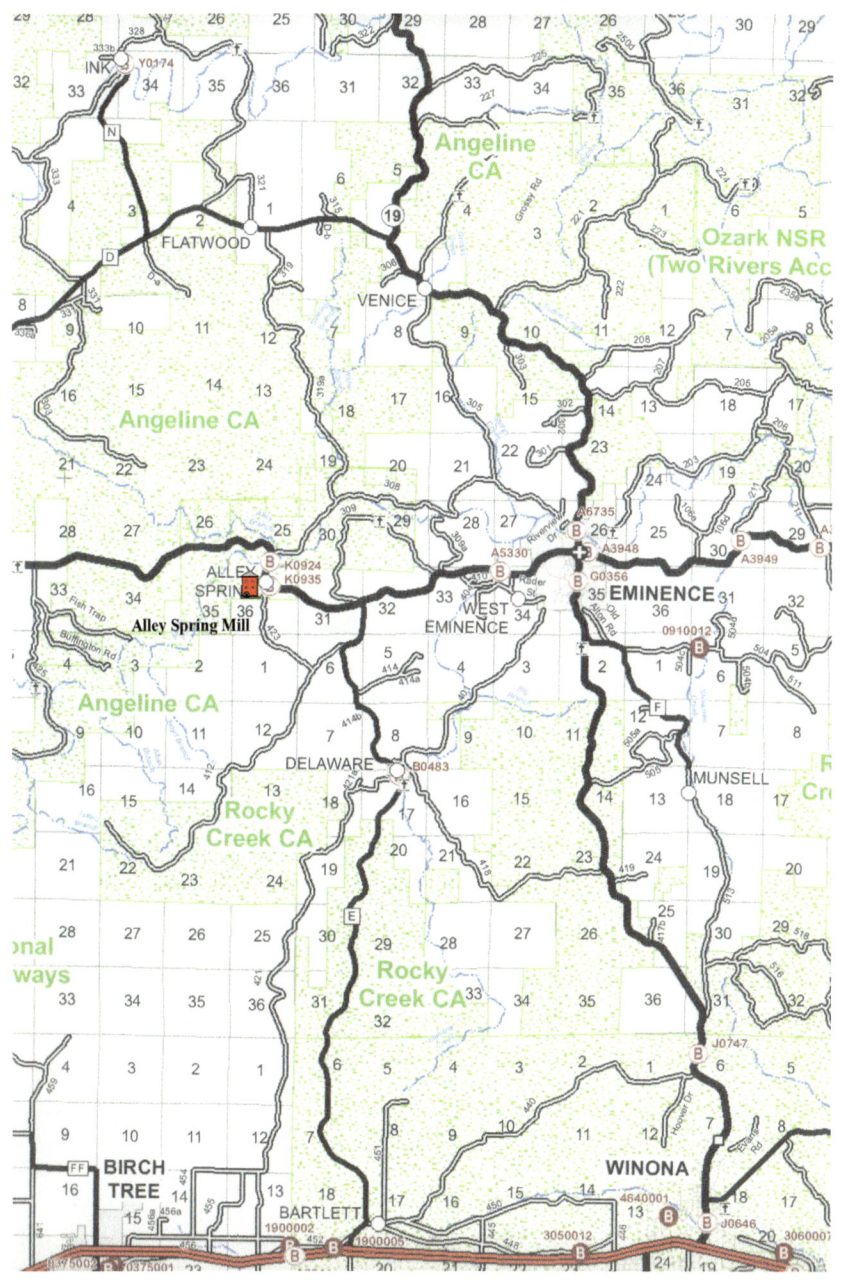

11

KLEPZIG MILL
SHANNON COUNTY

What do you get when you combine an old water mill, shut-ins (the rocks, not the people) and a tragedy? You get the historical and unique Klepzig Mill, located in Shannon County, Missouri, on Rocky Creek.

In the book, *Historic Ozarks Mills*, by Mike McCarthy, he wrote, "Klepzig Mill in Missouri's Shannon County is one of the most remote old mills in the nation." Indeed, it has possibly the most rocky road to traverse to get to the parking lot associated with the site, but the hike to the mill from the parking area is short and easy.

In 1912, Prussian Walter Klepzig bought the farm site that included a log cabin and a mill. He began improvements on the site, and according to the web resource *Clio*, "Klepzig built barbed and woven wire fences, purchased refined breeds of milk cows, and took advantage of outside marketing opportunities such as shipping cream to Beatrice, Nebraska, for processing." In 1928, he built the mill.

Klepzig ground corn and sawed logs at this site. Like other millers, he exercised his muscles and his mind to bring in more work and to serve his community. The logs he sawed went for his own use and for his neighbor's sawmill houses. According to the National Park Service website that features the Klepzig story, a sawmill house "was a building type that tended to replace log construction after the arrival of sawmills in a locale. A sawmill house could be erected quickly and by only one or two people. Instead of stud-wall framing, vertical planks were nailed to a hand-hewn sill at the bottom and a sawn two-by-four plate at the top. The resulting wall panels, fabricated flat on the ground, were then raised into place. Battens might then be added to cover the seams. Foundations were often piers of uncut and unmortared native stone." Klepzig didn't stop at supplying wood for homes, he also "routinely saved 'good boards'" for coffins.

People came from a 10-mile radius to grind their corn at this mill. History also reports that Klepzig showed compassion to those who could not afford to pay for their corn to be ground, and gave them free service. He also figured out how to harness the energy from the mill to run electricity to his farmstead.

According to *Clio*, the Klepzig Mill existed from about 1912 to 1934, during the "second of three instrumental periods of growth for the Southeast Missouri Ozarks referred to as the 'New South Ozarks.'" In fact, Clio supports my theory that Klepzig practiced advanced business practices as a forward-thinker regarding technology and meeting the needs of the community. The record shows that Klepzig owned the mill for 20 years, and throughout that time, he continued to improve its function – by upgrading the mill stones and adding a modern turbine to replace the mill's water wheel. Because of the prosperity of the mill, the Klepzig family purportedly owned the first radio in this area.

Klepzig sold the mill in 1931 to A.C. Brandt, an electrical equipment supplier from St. Louis. Brandt also made improvements to the mill site, but his ownership was during the period that saw a decline in the popularity of mills such as these small ones. Brandt did what many other mill owners turned to during this period – making the site attractive to anglers, hunters and recreationalists.

The mill is on the National Register of Historic Places.

The Shut-Ins

Many Missourians are familiar with shut-ins, namely Johnson's Shut-Ins and Rocky Falls Shut-Ins. According to Thomas R. Beveridge, in his book titled *Geologic Wonders and Curiosities of Missouri*, the term "shut-in" came from Appalachia and means gorge. When settlers from Appalachia came to the Ozarks, they applied this word combination to describe a stream that cuts through and between igneous rocks. Usually, valleys located above and below a set of shut-ins are wider than the shut-in. For some reason, a stream in a shut-in takes the more difficult route over the rocks, rather than the easier method of cutting itself a channel around the rocks.

The mill sits alongside Rocky Creek at the Mill Mountain Shut-ins, which are part of the National Scenic Riverways, east of Eminence, Missouri. When you visit this site, you can see the power of water. It's easy to imagine an entrepreneur, such as Klepzig, looking at the shut-ins and thinking, "I could use that water power." The creek gets narrower here, as shut-ins do, making the creek easier for Klepzig to harness, and the force from the drop in elevation of the water through the shut-ins naturally supplied power to turn water wheels and later, turbines. Concrete pieces of the raceway still stand, along with some of the original weir.

Even if people don't know about these shut-ins, if they hike along the Klepzig Mill Trail, part of The Ozark Trail (more than 390 miles), they will wander by this historic building. We saw a few hikers on the winter day that we visited the site.

According to McCarthy, during the operational years of the mill a child slipped and fell down the turbine shaft and died. McCarthy wrote, "I was told by one of the Klepzig descendants that it really never recovered [the mill] after the accident."

What to Do in the Area

The Klepzig Mill Trail is a six-mile, out-and-back hike that starts at Rocky Falls and traverses to the north on the aforementioned Ozark Trail. It passes through Buzzard Mountain and ends at Klepzig Mill and Rocky Creek. You may also fish in the creek, if you have a Missouri fishing license.

Visit the Klepzig Mill on the National Park Service website.

Find This Mill

Driving: To get there, From Winona, Mo, go 10 miles northeast on Highway H, then turn right on Highway NN. Go 5 miles to the pavement end (which is past the right turn for Rocky Falls Shut-ins), then turn left on County Road NN522, a gravel road. Go 1.1 miles to the mill, which will be on the right, and is partly obscured by trees. The road is dirt and not well maintained, and may be difficult for low-clearance vehicles.

lat 37.126560° N lon 91.198181° W

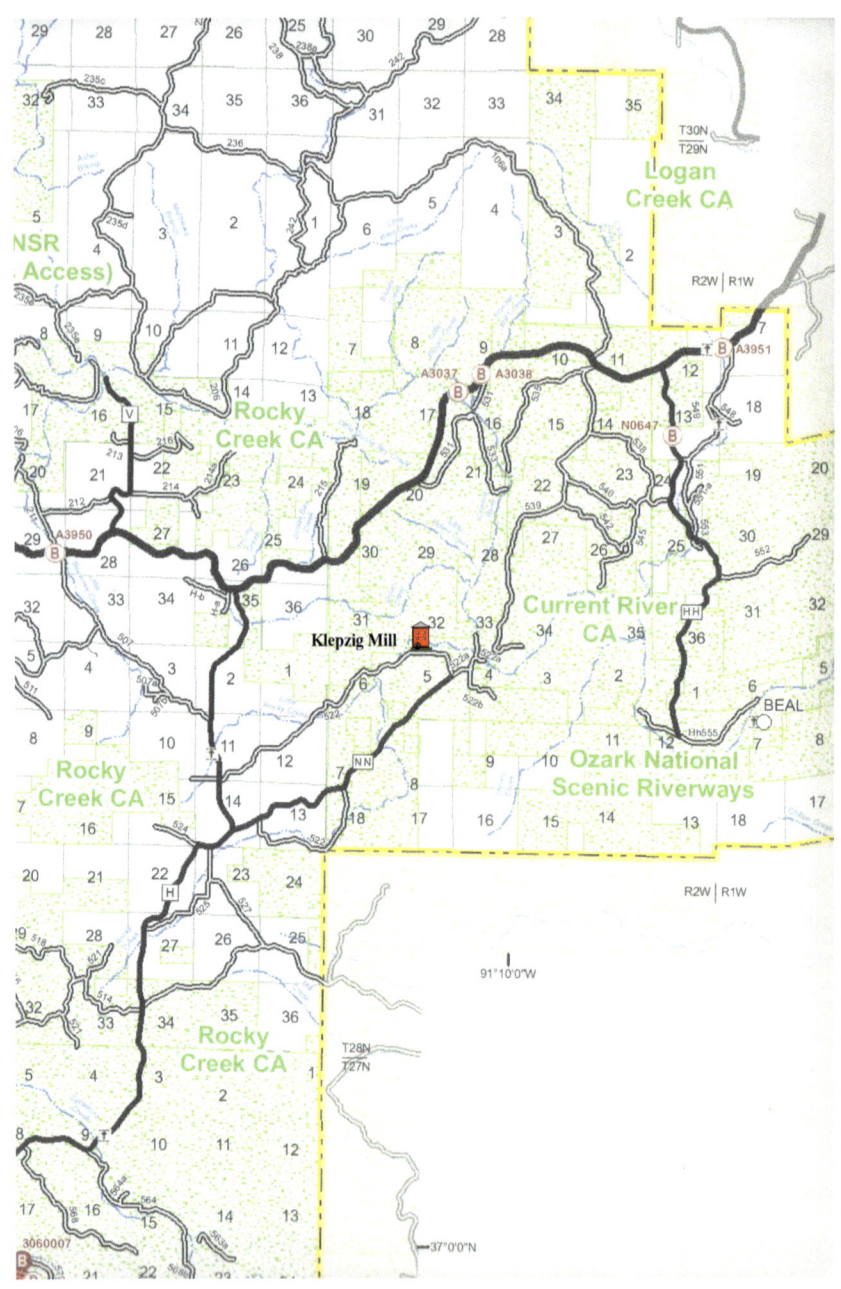

48

12

FALLING SPRING

OREGON COUNTY

When my sister visited here in the Ozarks a couple of years ago, we waltzed off to show her some of our favorite places, which of course, include mill sites. She told us she wanted to see a waterfall, and since Falling Spring is located within an easy drive from Alley Mill, we went. At the time, we noticed a sign posted stating that the old mill would be undergoing renovations. Even with COVID, the renovations obviously took place, and here's a little story about a revisit to Falling Spring.

The site sits in the vast Mark Twain National Forest, off Highway 19, in the Ozarks of Missouri. You'll have to drive on gravel roads to get to it, and they can be a bit rough and wet.

This old mill, built sometime between 1927 and 1929, is the second mill to sit on this site. At one time, there were two mills here. A head-race once ran from the spring that emerges from the bluff behind the mill, providing water power to an overshot wheel to grind corn, generate electricity and saw logs and make shingles. If you look closely, you can see some concrete up on the bluff that once formed the mouth of the chute for the water.

Actually, it is one of Missouri's youngest mills. You can also see concrete in the mill pond, which makes me wonder if the owners tried to keep fish onsite.

Some of the machinery is still onsite. Recent renovations have spruced up the place a bit.

Thomas Brown Cabin

Nearby, sits the Thomas Brown cabin, built in 1851 and kept intact. You'll notice the half-dovetail notches in the corners of the cabin, and if you step inside and look out the windows, you might be able to imagine what life was like back in the day. You can also hear the water nearby and view a pond with lily pads. During a springtime visit, daffodils bloomed like crazy near the spring and around the cabin. I like to imagine Mrs. Brown planted them back in the day.

The story goes that Thomas and Jane Brown homesteaded here. Hailing from Tennessee, they liked what they saw here and it reminded them of home.

There's even more to this story, though, thanks to an old *Ridge Runner* magazine that I found up in West Plains at the Old Time Flea Market Antiques Mall. From the Fall 1995 issue, there is an article about the Falling Springs Cemetery, located down the road from the mill. The article states that Thomas Brown served in the Confederate army and died in a Union prison camp near Rolla. His wife, Jane, is buried in this cemetery. Locals built the cemetery on the heels of an epidemic that occurred around the time of the Civil War, which supposedly took the lives of several unknown soldiers.

What to Do in the Area

Just down the road from Falling Spring is the New Liberty Civilian Conservation Camp (CCC) trail. The camp specialized in carpentry shops and classes, using native timber that had been cut from the nearby forest. Enrollees received carpentry training and built signs, picnic tables, tool boxes and fire caches. Some trainees also learned mechanic skills, necessary for keeping the various pieces of equipment and vehicles running. Along with milling services, the camp also contained a seedling storage house, and replanted at least 36,000 acres of pine in this region of the country. There's a trail that traverses through the woods. You'll get to smell the pines and also, imagine what life was like back then. You'll have to watch closely for the camp, as it lies in the woods on the way to Falling Spring.

Don't forget your fishing license and tackle! You may fish in the mill pond here.

Find This Mill

Falling Spring is located off Highway 19 about 9.6 miles south of Winona. Turn east (left) onto FR#3170 and bear left on FR #3164. Then, keep right at the next intersection, which is at about 2 miles. Go another .3 miles and you'll see the area. There are picnic tables at the site, and it's marked for day-use only.

lat 36.867548° N lon 91.295320° W

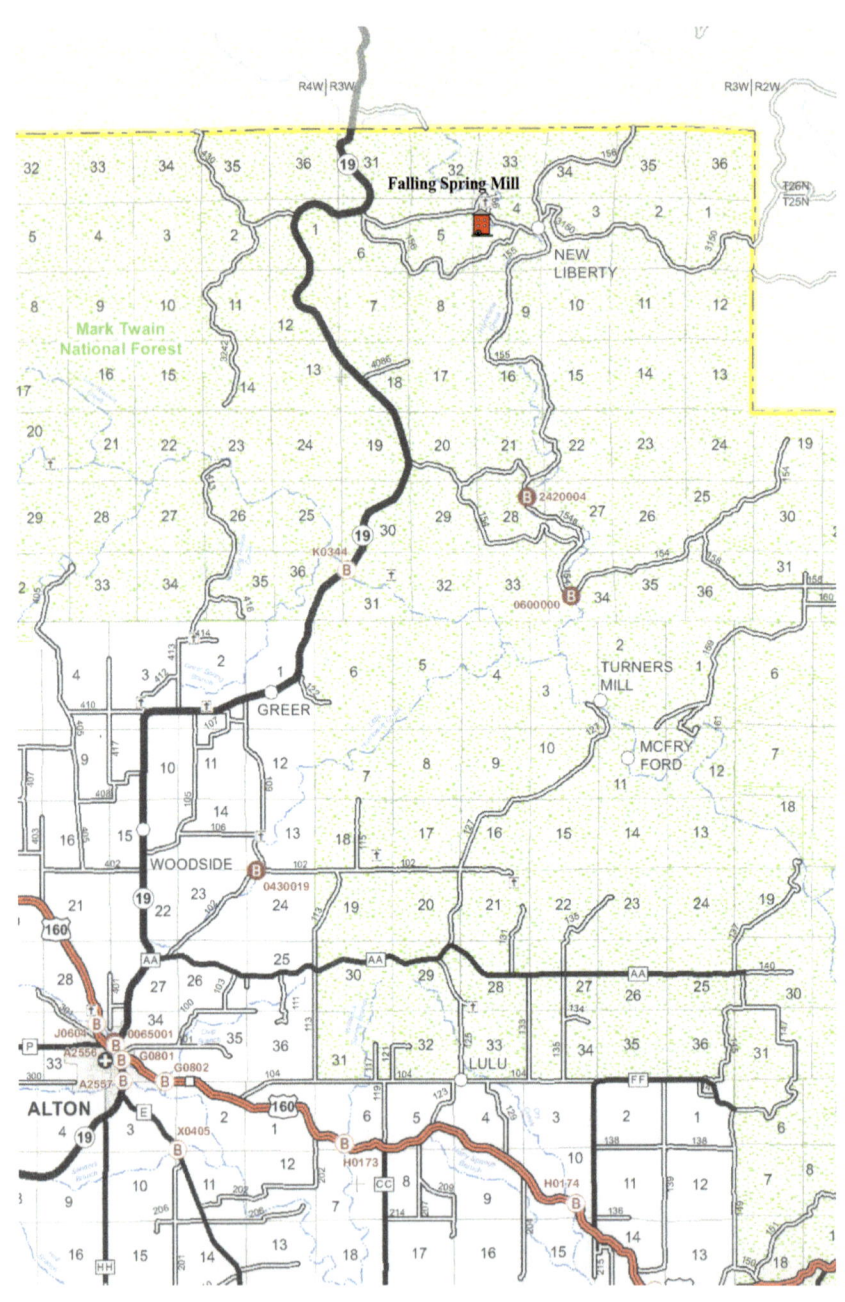

13

TURNER MILL
OREGON COUNTY

According to signage onsite, Turner Mill served the little village of Surprise, Missouri. The story goes that it acquired the name of Surprise because "of a village businessman's astonishment when a petition submitted by Jesse L. (Clay) Turner for a post office was accepted by the government."

In 1891, Turner purchased 160 acres and the spring. Fifty people lived in Surprise, and the post office sat in the back of the mill. Turner served as the postmaster, and also – as many millers did – ran a general store. He donated land and lumber to build the first school, and consequently, hired its first teacher, too. He also constructed a unique bridge over the Eleven Point River (past which the spring flows). Turner tipped the bridge upstream, which made the high water flood over it instead of against it. He died in 1933 and the school closed in 1945.

The first mill appeared in the 1850s, built by G. W. Decker. It used a wooden overshot wheel. Turner rebuilt the wheel in the 1890s, and made the old four-story mill building sing again. It also had a planer, drill press, saws and of course, grinding equipment. The mill ground wheat and corn.

According to signage, "The possession of enough power to operate the mill and maintenance of the wheel were ongoing concerns." Turner put in a turbine, but replaced it in 1915 with the 25-foot overshot wheel still present at the site. Oxen hauled the wheel to the mill. Oxen also pulled logs from the Eleven Point River to the mill to be sawed, since the roads ran rough-to-nonexistent back then.

Turner Mill Spring

The spring gushes forth from a high bluff, which you can climb up a trail to see. You might also spot what looks like old concrete foundation pieces across the way. The spring offers 1.5-million gallons a day on average.

What to Do in the Area

The sight is open all year, 24 hours a day, with a vault restroom in the parking lot area. Camping is available at Turner Mill South. Grills and tables and a lovely put-in point for boats (25-horsepower limit) can be found here. You may also fish.

Find This Mill

To see the Turner Mill overshot wheel, standing in the creek, you'll need to travel to the Turner Mill North River Access, located on the left side of the Eleven Point National Scenic River. You may access the wheel and spring via the trail system in place at Turner Mill North River Access, run by the US Forest Service.

Turner Mill North Picnic Area is accessed by hilly, gravel Forest roads 3152 and 3190. The turnoff to Turner Mill is 15 miles south of Winona or 11 miles north of Alton on Hwy 19. From Hwy 19, turn east onto FR 3152 for 6 miles then south on FR 3190 for 3 miles.

lat 36.766369° N lon 91.267113° W

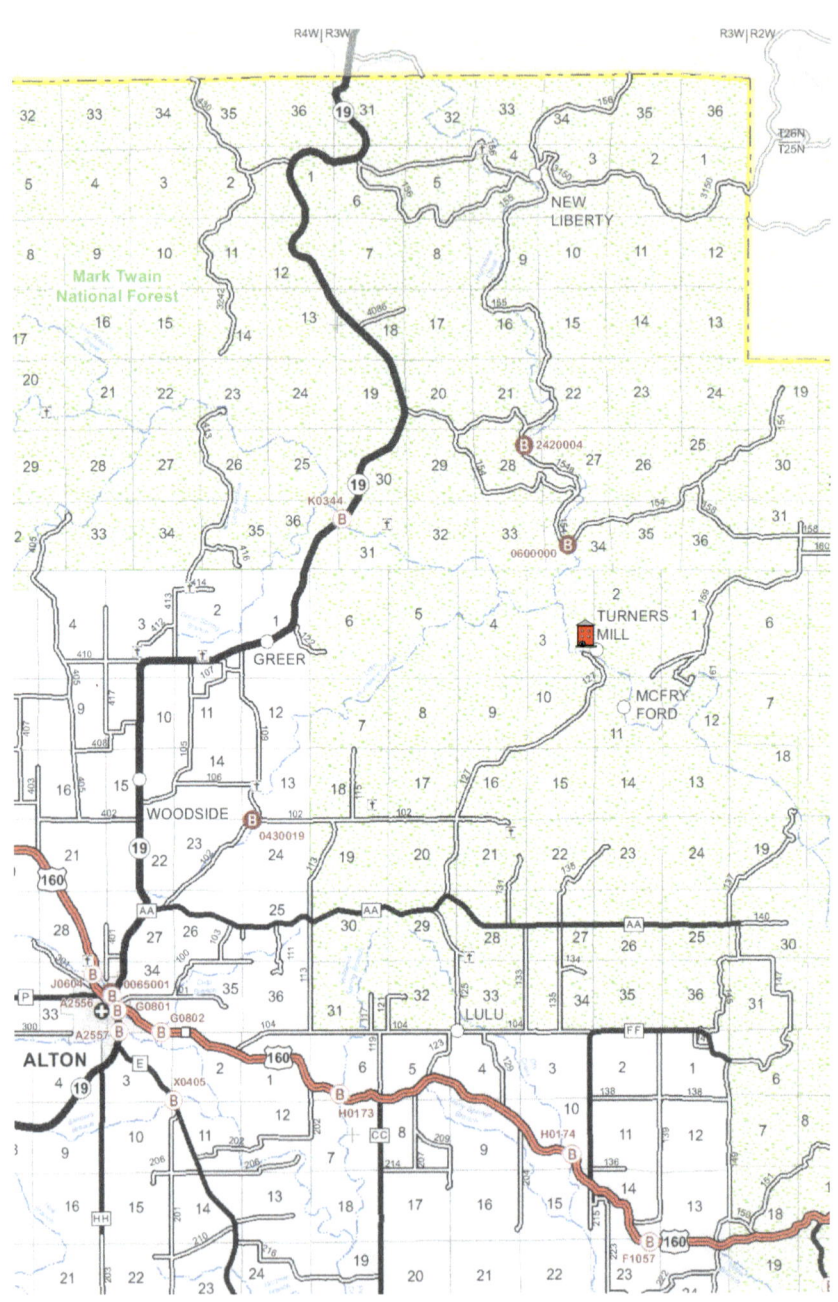

14

GREER MILL
OREGON COUNTY

On our way to Greer Spring, in Oregon County, Missouri, we drove by an old mill on a hill. It seemed an odd place to set a huge roller mill, and it looked as though it had been refurbished. We traversed the hike down to the spring, and drove back up the highway to the mill, parked and explored. It turns out we did exactly what those who have been instrumental in the restoration of Greer Mill wanted us to do, and ... they aren't finished yet.

Built in August 1860 by Samuel W. Greer, a Confederate Army captain, the mill fell victim to bushwhackers who set fire to it. Greer rebuilt it after the Civil War, down by the spring branch of Greer Spring – a 1.25-mile section of water that rushes to join the Eleven Point River. Of note, Greer Spring is the 10th largest spring in the US (on average 210-million gallons a day). Greer trained oxen to haul logs and grain on a circuitous hilly route – without a driver. In 1899, Greer installed a turbine at the spring branch and erected a new, three-story building uphill, on the present site. The new mill touted modern machinery that included pulleys and cables to transfer power from the turbine to the mill.

Greer sold half the interest of the mill in 1899 to George Mainprize, who operated the business until 1909. It changed hands a few times until it was sold to the Missouri Iron and Steel Corporation of St. Louis in 1919, that sold it to Louis E. Denning in 1922. In 1993, the U.S. Forest Service (USFS) purchased the property for 3.2 million, which included the spring and the mill site. Grants from Anheuser Busch and the Leo Drey (LAD Foundation) benefited the Service toward the purchase. It sits within the boundaries of the Mark Twain Forest. Part of the deal included 20 years of recreational use for the Denning family.

And, that's where the restoration story starts. In 2013, at the end of the term of the Dennings' use of the property, the mill became the focus of several interested residents of Oregon County. They formed the Friends of the Eleven Point River, a non-profit organization, for restoring the old mill. Brian Sloss, president of Friends of the Eleven Point, described the renovation process, which involved HistoriCorps. HistoriCorps is a service learning organization that partners with the U.S. Forest Service and Dept. of Agriculture to preserve historic sites on public lands. Between 2014 and 2015, in the summer, HistoriCorps completed the first phase restoration, along with help from Passport In Time and the Mark Twain National Forest.

According to HistoriCorps online, "The work included reconstruction of the structural members on the west elevation, rebuilding and repointing the foundation on the west elevation, residing the west elevation to a height of 8 inches above grade, stabilizing an interior bent, and minor repair of stairs and infill of window openings." It replaced interior posts and timbers, cleaned the interior (which had been vandalized), excavated by hand to improve drainage on the east side of the mill and they also improved the drainage situation in the basement, replaced wall framing and sill plates.

The Friends of the Eleven Point organization also volunteered onsite, and hired local Amish workers. Sloss said the workmen did the following tasks during that time: added a new roof, replaced the floor – which included working with a local flooring company to cut the flooring to the specific size and style of the times, hired Amish to build and install windows and shutters (again, according to the period) and replaced the siding.

In 2016, HistoriCorps completed phase #3 of the process to restore Greer Mill, which included finishing the stabilization work and rebuilding the loading dock in the front.

Sloss says the building is only open for special occasions and that the Friends have held fundraisers with open houses. Sloss said the LAD Foundation has been helpful with funds, as well as other grant monies. The Friends also have hosted trivia nights, and held auctions, silent auctions and canoe races to raise funds for restoration. Donations are always welcome.

Parking remains dicey, and the location of the building on a hilltop immediately off the highway is another problem; the Missouri Department of Transportation does not give parking access at the site. The Friends of the Eleven Point hope that a path may someday be cut from the parking lot of the spring access area up to the mill site.

Visit Friends of the Eleven Point River online to see more information about this lovely old mill in Missouri. Also, follow Friends of the Eleven Point River on Facebook, which is especially useful for events and updates.

What to Do in the Area

Falling Spring Mill is just down the road from this site, so you could take in two mills in one day.

Find This Mill

From Alton, turn left on Highway 19 north. Go 8 miles and the parking area for Greer Spring and Trail will be on your left. Continue on Highway 19 for .5 mile to Greer Mill, which is on a hill on the left. There's a small (unapproved) parking area.

lat 36.786560° N lon 91.342457° W

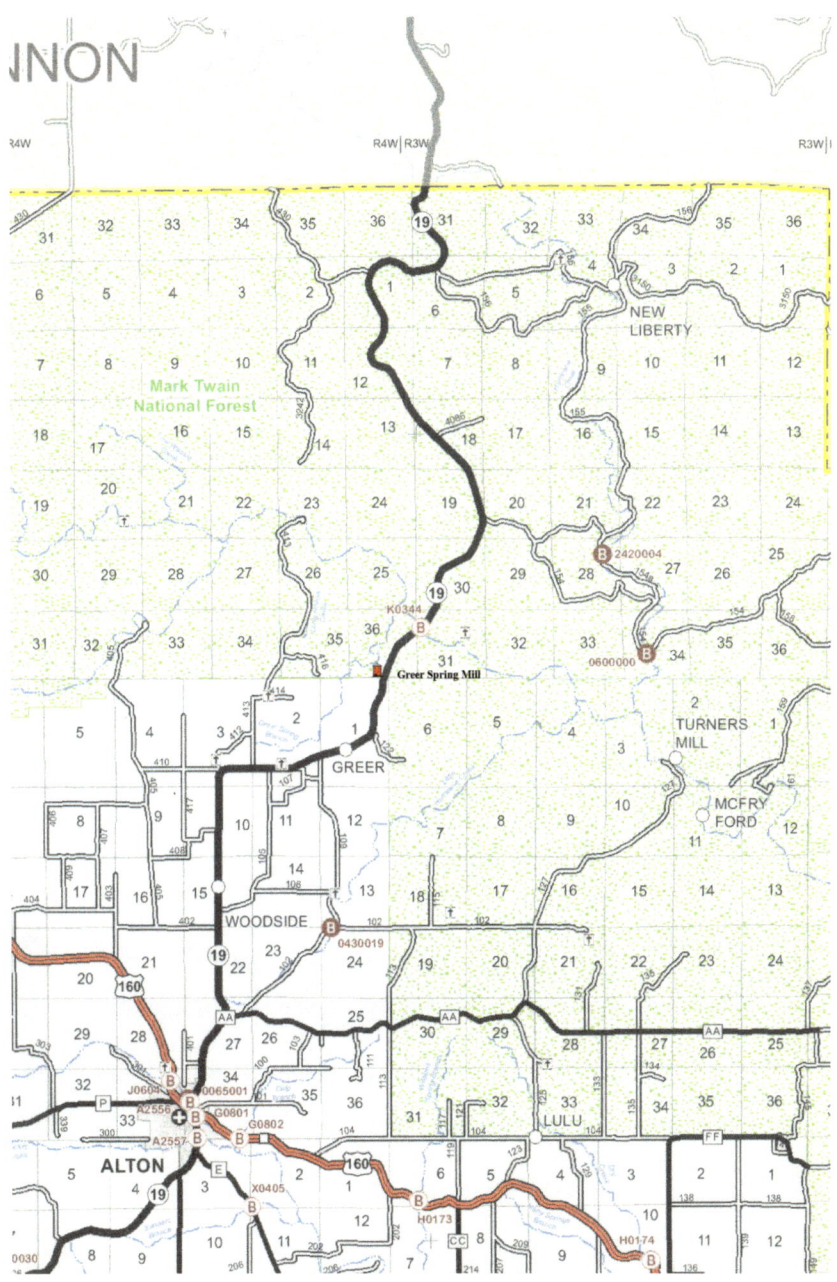

15

TOPAZ MILL
DOUGLAS COUNTY

Topaz Mill stands in a holler in Douglas County, a perfect representation of what a gristmill should look like, complete with a gushing spring nearby and a raceway. Next door to the mill, stands an associated general store.

Neither of these buildings would be here had it not been for the energy and foresight of Joe O'Neal. Joe's nephew, Joe Bob O'Neal, who lives onsite now, said his uncle bought this place in 1957. "When they bought this place, both of the buildings were in bad shape," he recalled. "The siding was falling off and there wasn't any glass in any of the windows and when my uncle had time and money, he got them closed in to keep the weather and varmints out."

Joe Bob O'Neal stands outside Topaz Mill, looking over the raceway.

Little by little, year by year, Joe Bob's uncle repaired and shored up the mill and general store, and even added paint to the store (which had never seen paint). Joe Bob spent some happy childhood days running on the grounds of this property, and now, a retired railroad worker, he loves to spend his time on a dirt bike on the 400-acre property.

Topaz Mill is a place where my husband used to retreat to from high school days, playing hooky and swimming in the mill pond. About 18 miles south of Mountain Grove, the mill site is believed to have first been appreciated for its merits in about 1840, when Aaron and Alabeth Freeman settled near the spring and built the first grist mill.

Topaz also offered an onsite grocery store, barber shop, cannery blacksmith shop and the most important place – a post office. Supposedly, the postmaster chose the name "Topaz," not for the color of the spring (although on the day that we saw it, we noticed a topaz circle in the center of the spring where the water bubbled up), but because Topaz hadn't been chosen for a Missouri place name yet.

According to *Water Mills of the Missouri Ozarks*, by George G. Suggs, Jr., the mill changed ownership several times between the deaths of the Freemans and purchase by Robert Hutcheson in 1890. Hutcheson and his wife, Mary, had great plans for the mill, and moved it farther from the spring, directing the water to energize the turbines via a dam and flume. In 1895, construction began on the three-story building that would grind not only flour, but also, corn.

I love that the mill is painted cherry red. That's classic. Bits and pieces of operating machinery lie nearby, and the turbine and its associated housing and machinery are still attached to the building at the back. Fed by a 10-million-gallon-per-day spring of the same name, the current mill was constructed in 1895. It employed modern technology of the times that took advantage of a nearby raceway.

Joe Bob and his wife, Betsy, started a non-profit organization, Friends of Topaz Mill, Inc., with a Facebook page. It accepts donations for preservation and maintenance purposes. I recommend that you call ahead, since the mill sits on private property. You might even arrange for a tour.

Find This Mill

Topaz Mill is in Douglas County. From Mountain Grove, Missouri, take MO Highway 95 South to MO Highway 76. Turn left, go 5-6 miles to EE, then take a right on EE then go approx. 2.5 miles. Take a left on County Road 274 and follow for a little more than a mile. You'll see Topaz Mill down in a beautiful holler.

lat 36.946084° N lon 92.203134° W

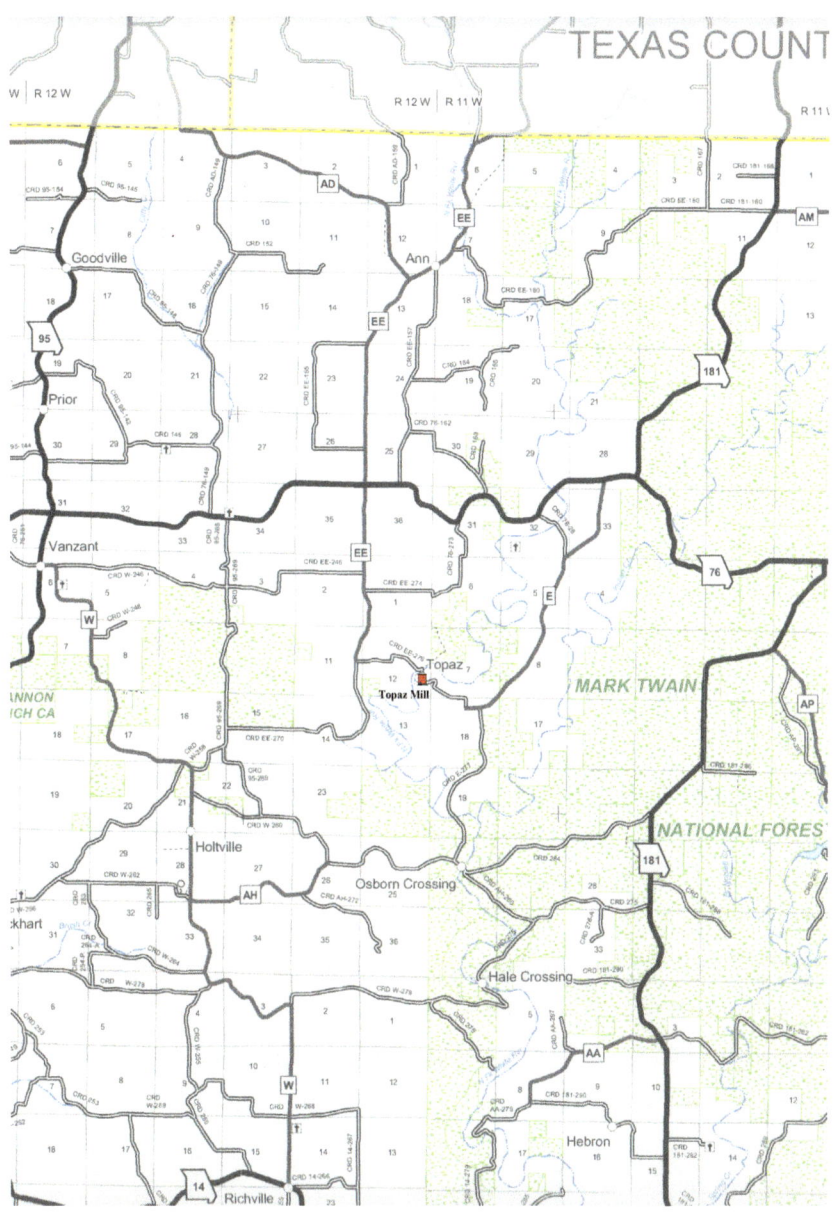

16

HODGSON MILL

OZARK COUNTY

This lovely mill stands near Dora, off Route 181. I've never seen anyone else onsite here, but the property is open to the public for viewing. The building is not open, but you don't need to go inside to appreciate its history. In fact, you might be acquainted with some of its products, labeled Hodgson-Aid Mill, in grocery stores all around the country and at Amazon. Hodgson Mill is headquartered in Effingham, Illinois, but began here in the Ozarks sometime around 1837.

The first gristmill was destroyed during the Civil War, and had been built on Bryant Creek in 1861 by William Holeman. Somehow, Alva Hodgson acquired title to the property in 1884, and built another mill. The current mill, in all its red glory, and near a limestone bluff from which the spring flows that powers the mill, was built in 1897. Hodgson built a state-of-the-art mill with two Leffel turbines and roller mills. The flour had a more refined texture to it than previous millings offered.

Hodgson sold his interest in the mill to his brother, George, and built nearby Dawt Mill in 1899. Later, ownership passed to Charles Aid. Thereby, it's known as the Hodgson-Aid Mill. It had other owners throughout the ensuing years, who expanded the line of products to include cornmeal, bran and other flours, and who also ran a canoe operation and antiques store from the site. By 1976, production of flour took place down in a facility in Gainesville, because the mill couldn't keep up with the demand for its goods. Other owners tried to keep the mill running as a tourist stop, and flooding didn't help matters.

While searching for more information about Hodgson Mill, I discovered House Resolution No. 077C.01, from 2003, that acknowledged the achievement of Hank and Jean Macler, of Tecumseh, who are responsible for restoration of the Hodgson-Aid Mill. They bought it in 2001. The Maclers renovated the mill with the help of Amish craftsmen, and received the 2003 Preserve Missouri Award for Rural Preservation.

According to an article in *The Columbus Dispatch*, Hodgson Mill's three-story section is 95 percent original. The article also reported that energy from the water's movement powered sewing machines for the first Big Smith Overalls factory in the 1930s, located in the back of the mill.

The last owners on record are John and Gwen Deakle, who bought the mill in 2011.

Obviously, whoever owns it doesn't mind if people stop and visit it. And it's well worth seeing. The creek, the old bridge, the beautiful bluff and of course, the historical mill, blend together to allow your imagine to harken back to times when life revolved around this type of industry.

What to Do in the Area

About 1000 feet away from Highway 181, below the low water bridge over Bryant Creek at Hodgson Mill is the Sycamore Access, where the public may fish, swim or put in canoes and kayaks to float the upper Bryant.

Find This Mill

Hodgson Mill is located 17 miles northeast of Gainesville, Missouri, on Highway 181.

lat 36.709704° N lon 92.266497° W

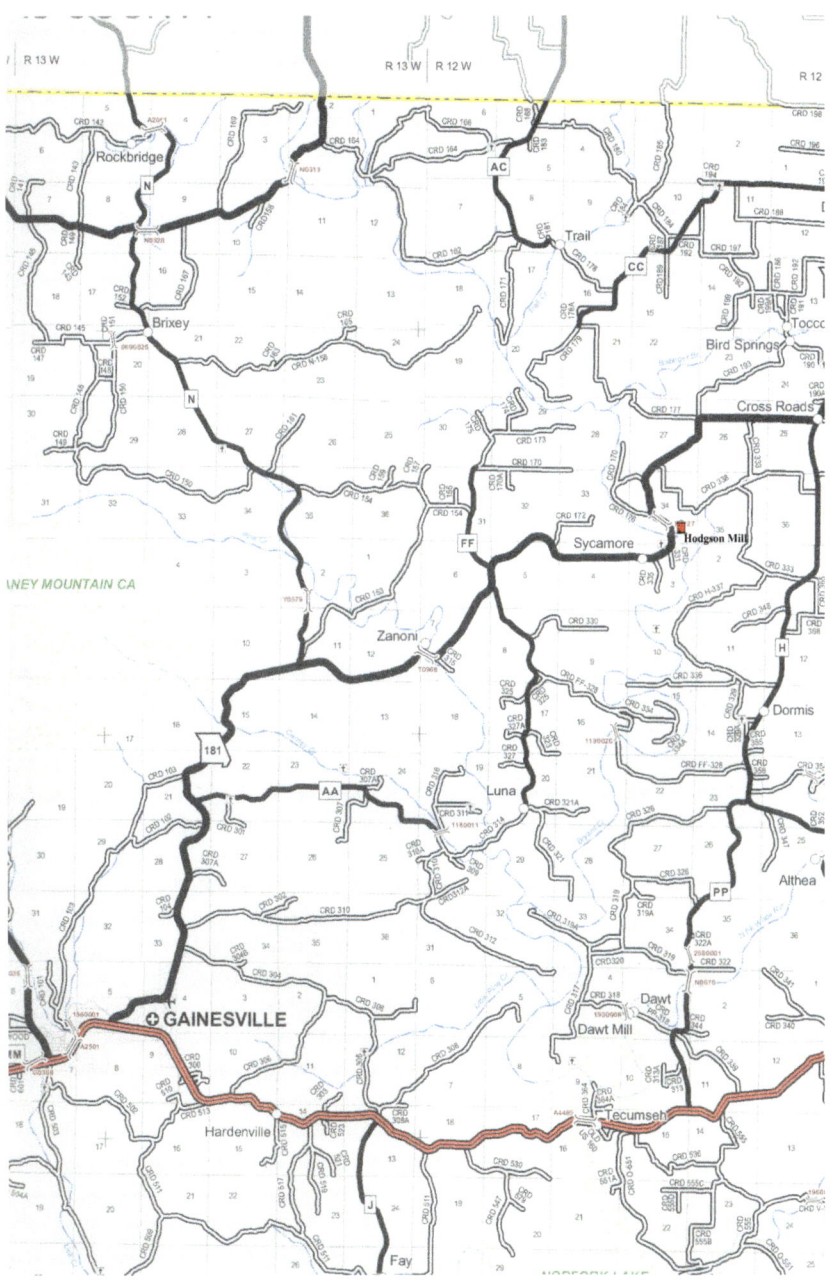

17

DAWT MILL
OZARK COUNTY

As I've mentioned, Ozark County is home to many mills – Rockbridge, Zanoni, Hodgson, Hammond and Dawt.

My first trip to Dawt happened about 20 years ago during a conference, and it included a float trip. I remember being intrigued by the mill's history and its massive presence on the North Fork of the White River.

The history of the mill includes angst, bankruptcy, divorce, flooding and death. The mill's title changed hands many time since its start in 1866. The land where the mill stands today was once part of a land grant (homestead) under Pres. Ulysses S. Grant in 1874 to Ruhama J. Isom.

It has been speculated that Isom ran a mill on the property for several years before acquiring the deed. Owner John C. Caldwell began building the present-day mill in 1892 and employed a popular designer of mills, L.A. Rogers, who oversaw the work. A tragedy occurred when Rogers drowned in the millpond in 1893.

Years later, one of its proprietors included Alva Hodgson, who owned another mill (Hodgson Mill) over on Bryant Creek. He and members of his family purchased this property in January 1901. By 1906, the site included the three-story mill, general store with a blacksmith shop, sawmill and cotton gin. The next year, Hodgson opened a post office, and called it "Dawt."

Some have surmised that Dawt is a word combination of D and A from "dam," and W and T from "water." From this time until the mid-1960s, the mill kept "grinding away." When acquired by Wayne and Ruth Dinnell in 1966, the site blossomed into a tourist attraction. The Dinnells rented out campsites, and ground cornmeal, which they offered for sale at the mill. At this time, they added an ornamental mill wheel to the building to add to the ambience. Later owners saw the attraction of the site to tourists and continued offering recreational opportunities to interested parties.

The present-day owners, Dr. Ed Henegar and his wife, Mary, also envisioned the site (purchased in 1995) as a resort/vacation place. With restaurants, meeting rooms, watersports and lodging, the property can accommodate a personal weekend getaway or a small conference for business purposes.

The Henegars have seen trying times surrounding the mill, especially in the forms of tragedy, flood and fire. According to an article in the *Ozark County Times*, flooding earlier in August 2013 removed a 12-foot section of the dam. In June 2016, 13-year-old Chloe Butcher from Springfield drowned after being sucked underwater near a break in the old dam's center. Purportedly, the teenage girl had been trying to help another child who eventually got sucked through the dam and rescued on the other side.

Dr. Henegar was onsite and pronounced her dead, after her body had been recovered. Dawt Mill's owners applied to the Army Corps of Engineers to remove the dam structure shortly after the drowning, in July 2016. *The Springfield News-Leader* reported another problem with taking down the dam: "Dr. Ed Henegar, owner of Dawt Mill, said he wasn't sure when the project would begin. Aside from the dam's age — it was built in 1892 and partially collapsed three years ago — the dam might have endangered hellbender salamanders living in it, which could complicate the dam's destruction." By March 2017, and after approval of the Army Corps of Engineers and the U.S. Fish and Wildlife Service, and by enforcing provisions from the federal Clean Water Act, removal of the dam began. All in all, 290 feet of the 420-foot structure was removed.

In April 2017, Missouri saw historic flooding, and it affected Dawt Mill greatly. In fact, it wiped away many of the features I saw while onsite in April 2016 for a craft fair.

After rebuilding from the flood, the Henegars' mill again underwent another setback when in September 2022, a fire started in the kitchen and spread to other parts of the mill. I saw some of the smoke damage that was still evident in the beams of the structure while onsite in April 2023.

However, as has been Dawt's history, the Henegars rolled up their sleeves and also, hired contractors to restore the site. Today, Dawt Mill offers lodging in the form of a variety of cabins, camping and RV spots, floating opportunities (with canoes, kayaks, rafts) along with opportunities that include Hearthside Dining and The Beach Bar.

The mill's website and Facebook page list other attractions, such as drives and hikes, that people may enjoy while staying at Dawt.

Find This Mill

Dawt Mill is located at 8 Dawt Mill Drive, Tecumseh, Missouri.
lat 39.609821° N lon 92.278062° W

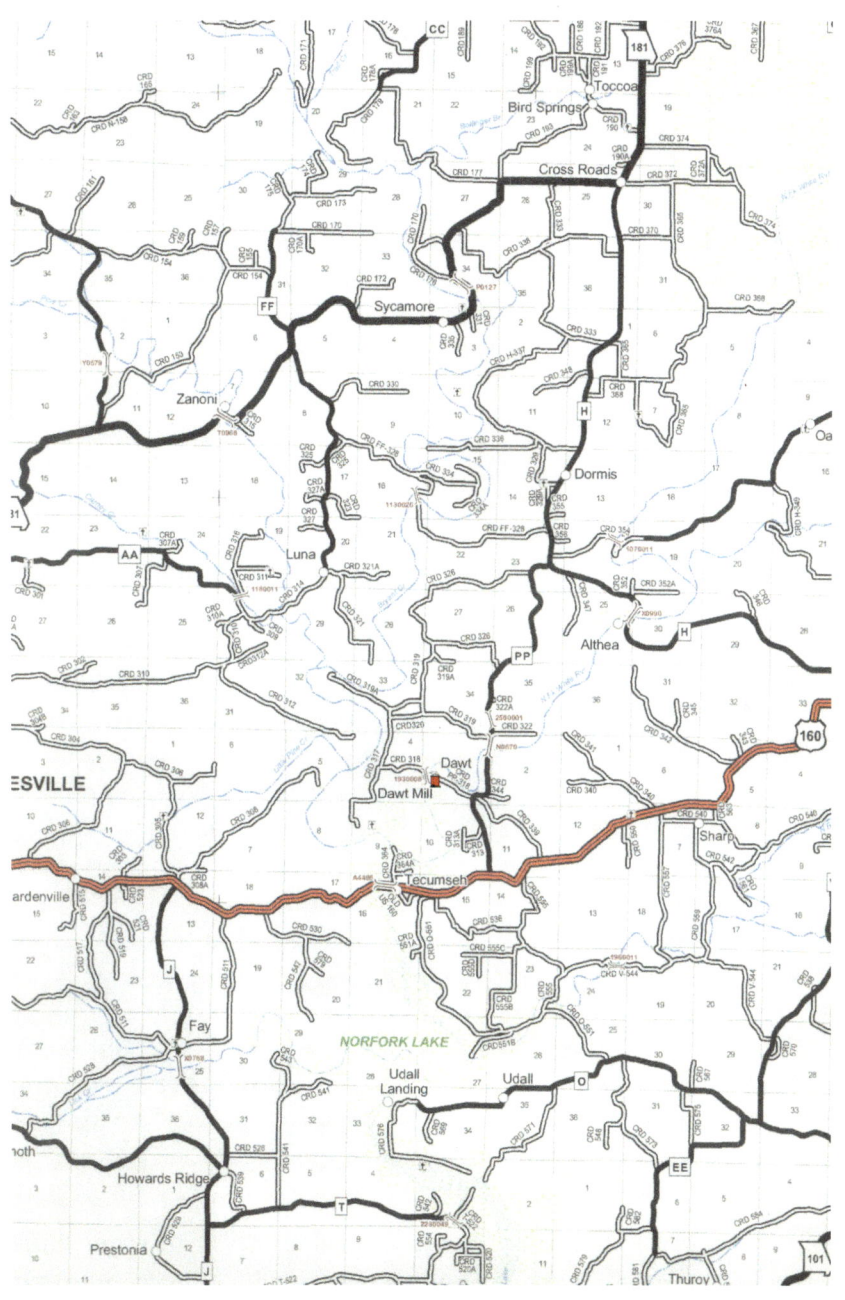

18

ZANONI MILL

OZARK COUNTY

The Ozarks of Missouri are home to a wide variety of water mills from bygone days. Ozark County is home to five of these mills that can still be seen: Rockbridge, Hodgson, Dawt, Hammond and Zanoni. Zanoni Mill is now an event center and owned privately.

Although stripped of most of its indoor machinery and mill properties, the renovated Zanoni Mill touts a rich history. The first mill onsite is believed to have existed before the Civil War. The Ozark County Chamber of Commerce claims, "Milling began at Zanoni during Civil War days in a little mud-built cabin built by John Cody." No one knows whether the mill site survived the war or was, as several other mills had been, burned at that time.

According to information in *A History of Ozark County, 1841-1991*, which I purchased on CD at the Ozark County Historium, two men – George Schoemaker and John Cody – bought the property in the late 1890s because a mill onsite had burned. The book states this mill is the only "true water mill" in Ozark County, because of its overshot wheel, as compared to the other mills' turbines. The men built a new mill that harnessed the energy from a nearby hillside spring, averaging 194,000 gallons of water a day. To this day, you can see the wooden flume that channeled water to the mill and turned the overshot wheel. Schoemaker added a sawmill to the site, too.

In 1898 Schoemaker served as the postmaster for the Zanoni post office, named after Zanoni, Virginia. However, Zanoni was also the name of the protagonist in an Edward Bulwer-Lytton novel from 1842 titled *Zanoni: A Rosicrucian Tale*.

Fire again destroyed this mill in 1904, but it didn't damage the wheel, flint mill stones or machinery. Schoemaker and Cody sold to A.P. Morrison and W.E. Newton in 1905. Morrison built the mill that you see today, and he also added French buhrstones that could grind 20 bushels of corn or graham flour per day.

After this mill began seeing success, a community formed – as they oft do – around the property. Morrison, like other entrepreneurs who owned mill sites – took advantage of the popularity of the site and built a store, blacksmith shop and cotton gin. He charged 1/8-measure for work done at the mill.

By 1921, Morrison had built a water-powered generator that allowed him to operate the mill and store's lights, along with 10 industrial sewing machines for sewing overalls (on the second floor of the mill). The overalls operation was an affiliate site for Dr. M.C. Amyux, who owned an overall factory in West Plains, using the "Blue Jay" label.

Morrison also rebuilt the overshot wheel in the late 1940s. Unfortunately, the wheel served the mill for only a few years, before the mill closed in 1951. Morrison kept the general store open until his death in 1969.

In 1973, the Gramex Corporation of Hazelwood bought the property from the Morrison estate. The corporation renovated the mill and store.

In 1976, Dave Morrison, grandson of A.P. Morrison, bought the property from Gramex, essentially bringing it back into the family. Morrison and his wife, Mary, ran a cattle operation, built a big colonial home and a reflecting pool near the mill. Water from the pool runs over a spillway and into Pine Creek. They ran a bed-and-breakfast establishment onsite, as well. The Morrisons sold the property to Bruce and Kimberly Peters in 2005. Later, Kansas City cattle ranchers Scott and Becky Matthews purchased it from the Peters' family in 2012. Currently, the site is called Zanoni Mill Ranch, and not only offers the old mill as a venue for gatherings and weddings, but also sells Black Angus beef from the ranch.

I met the present day owners onsite in May 2021 and they allowed us to take photos of the mill and store. It is a gorgeous drive to the site, as well.

What to Do in the Area

In fact, you may want to make a day of it and tour all the mills in this area. Rockbridge, Zanoni, Hodgson, Hammond and Dawt are all within a 21-mile radius (driving distance) of Gainesville.

You may see more about what present-day Zanoni offers on its Facebook page. I recommend that you contact the Matthews before driving to their home.

Find This Mill

Zanoni Mill, is located nine miles northeast of Gainesville on Highway 181.

lat 36.686704° N lon 92.331729° W

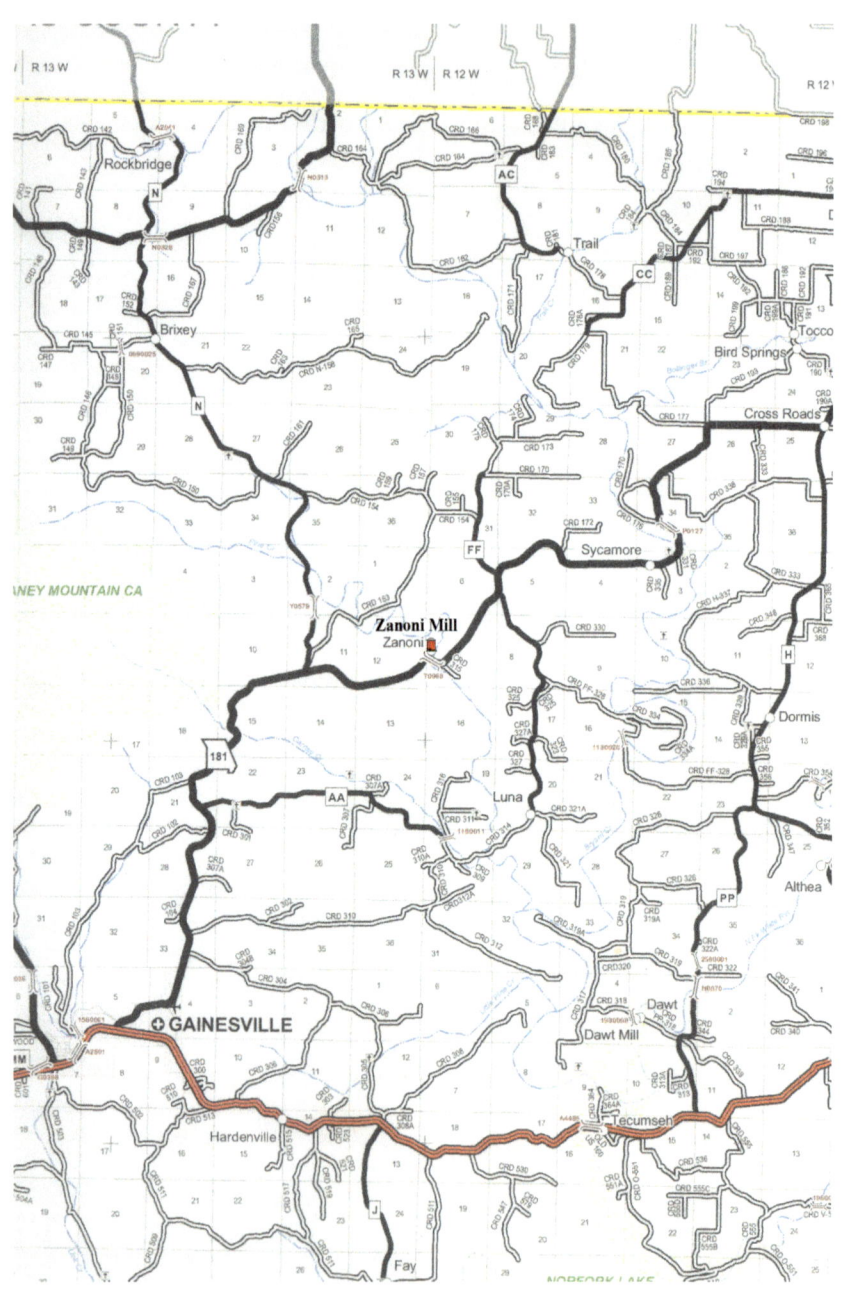

19

ROCKBRIDGE MILL
OZARK COUNTY

Technically called the Rockbridge Trout & Game Ranch, this historic setting comes with a rich history that began in 1841, when a few families left Kentucky with three wagonloads, led by Capt. Kim Amyx. After six months and 500 miles, they found their new home, which actually is near another mill (Hodgson).

They established a town called Rockbridge, located near where

Spring and Bryant Creeks meet. During the Civil War, fire destroyed the town and mill.

B.V. Morris built today's grist mill in 1868 a few miles from the original site, and shortly after that, according to the Rockbridge website, it gained a "post office, a general store, Masonic Lodge, bank, church, school, blacksmith shop, and a large farm house, known today as the White House." As with most mills during that time, it served as the center of the universe for people who brought grain to be milled. People also voted at this location.

The mill ground white "patent" flour, traditional cornmeal and graham flour. Patent flour is finely ground and comes with a high starch content.

By the end of the 1930s, technology brought the end of the need for this type of milling and blacksmithing. The mill closed in 1948. In the late 1940s, the Amyx family moved back to its homesite and ran a sawmill here, and an auto company in Gainesville. In 1954, they hatched an idea to reinvent the mill and general store/post office as Rockbridge Rainbow Trout & Game Ranch. They negotiated the sale of land and buildings in the village, including the mill, store, bank, church and two houses. Until it was recently closed, due to cost-saving attempts by the Postal Service, it was the oldest working post office in the county.

The Amyx family donated sweat equity to build the fish hatchery fed by the mill stream, which rears more than 200,000 lovely rainbow trout annually. As well as the successes garnered by the family, they suffered tragedy when after a fish delivery in Tennessee in 1966, Edd Amyx was electrocuted.

In 1986, the old store succumbed to a fast-burning fire. The family rebuilt the facility quickly that year, but according to an article in *The Ozark County Times*, had no record of who had made reservations for the resort. If a guest appeared and claimed to have made a reservation and there wasn't a vacancy, he or she would be invited home to stay with a family member.

The facilities, which sit on 2000+-acres, offer a gun club with sporting clays and 5-stand courses. As for fishing (for a fee), you can almost be assured of catching big, beautiful rainbow trout. Staff will clean and filet the fish for you to take home afterward. Fishing guides are available for hire.

The restaurant – I saved the best for last – is worth the trip just for the meal. Set in the old general store, the last time I was there it served trout 20 different ways, along with a full menu and bar. Or, you can ask the kitchen to cook your trout that you've caught, if you want to stay and eat. That would be a great treat.

You may also wander around the mill site, and even check the underside of the building where the turbine machinery used to reside. It's a quiet, calm place to visit, and you'll enjoy the view of the old mill and river from the dining room of the restaurant. Stop for awhile and order up a drink at the Grist Mill Club, an old pub inside the mill overlooking the mill pond. I always enjoy watching families catching fish here, and indeed, our own family has benefitted from this opportunity in the past. You may also order a snack or meal from the restaurant to be brought over to the bar area.

Watch for special events annually at this location, including Fourth of July and Christmas with Santa. If you really want to get away, stay onsite in one of the houses, rooms, suites or condos at Rockbridge.

Visit Rockbridge Rainbow Trout & Game Ranch, Inc., at its website.

What to Do in the Area

If you want to fish in a public stream, check out Spring Creek. Don't forget about shooting an easy-to-traverse sporting clays course, set in the beautiful woods, at the nearby Rockbridge Gun club.

Find This Mill

Rockbridge Mill is located at 4297 County Road 142.
lat 36.788955° N lon 92.408900° W

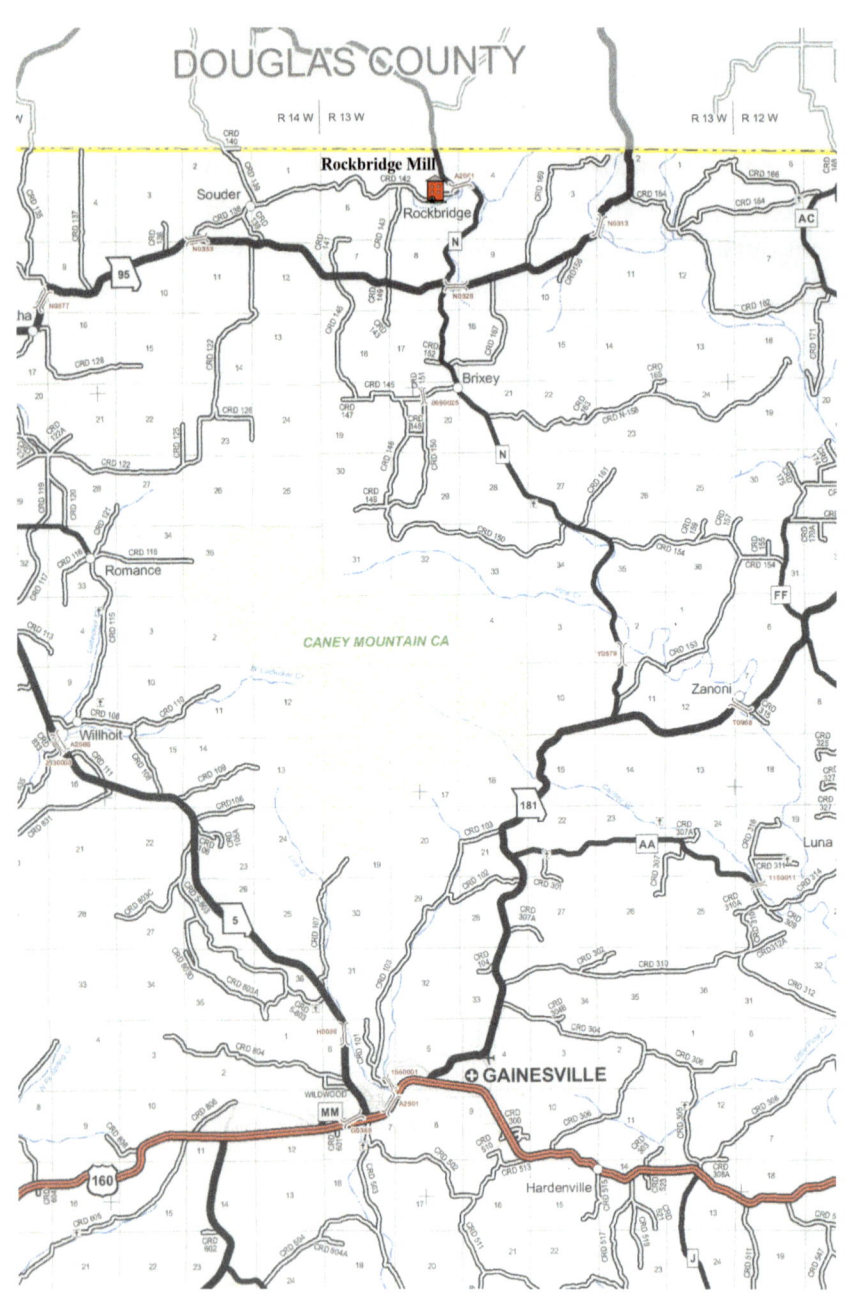

20

HAMMOND MILL

OZARK COUNTY

Whenever we plan on heading out to explore the Ozarks, I check to see if there might be an old mill standing somewhere near where we're planning to go. We decided to explore the Hercules Glades Wilderness a while ago, and also, to find Hammond Mill because it's just down the road.

Hammond Mill

At the time we visited the mill (Oct. 2020), it stood forlorn and for sale. I called the real estate agency listed on the sign and an agent gave us permission to photograph the mill and be on the property. The mill was listed along with five acres of land. Because of some modern day renovations to convert the mill into a lodge for hunters, there are some comforts, such as three full baths. We peeked in the windows, and it appears that completing this project will require vision and a fat bank account.

At the time of the printing of this book, rumor has it that the old mill has been sold and is being renovated to make a home for a family.

The mill sits right off the country gravel road, formerly (according to Phyllis Rossiter, in *The Mills of Ozark County*) "the old, Jacksonport Salt Road, a main route betwee [sic] Springfield, Mo. and Jacksonport, Ark. during the Civil War."

In another good resource, *Water Mills of the Missouri Ozarks*, by George G. Suggs, Jr., the author writes that Hammond Mill stood near a site specifically chosen for a village by S.J. Williams, John Squires and Jon W. Grudier. The nearby Little North Fork of the White River – when dammed – provided power for the water mill.

Grudier built the present three-story mill in 1907. It churned out flour, meal and food for livestock and took in wheat and corn from the surrounding area. It sold its flour under the brand Ozarks Queen Flour. Suggs writes that at times the mill ran 24-hour shifts, especially during the harvest season. Underwater turbines powered rollers and millstones. According to Suggs, by 1908 the town of Hammond had grown up around the mill and included a whiskey distillery, post office, drugstore, two general stores and a bank. Supposedly, the mill operated until 1940.

When Suggs visited the mill back in the late 1980s, he noted the destruction of the underside of the mill from wind and water damage. Floods had shifted the stream bed away from the mill, too. It's like nature and mankind moved away from this place.

Rossiter also wrote something about the old water mills that I believe embodies why so many people love to visit these pieces of our Ozarks past: "We come away convinced that the Ozarks water mill is historical – and living proof that man's industry needn't destroy, but can become one with his environment. And as long as these old mills still stand, we'll go on straddling that barrier that is so much the essence of the Ozarks."

What to Do in the Area

Part of the Mark Twain National Forest, Hercules Glades Wilderness contains 12,413 acres of rugged land in Taney County of southwest Missouri. While visiting the Wilderness, we drove on a couple of roads that border its southern edge – Blair Ridge and Cane Creek, each having several trailheads for hiking or horseback riding – that provided spectacular views, along with cloistered forest lanes. If you want to see a wide variety of trees and other native plants, this area has it. In fact, you may download a map of Hercules Glades Wilderness online.

As we continued south out of the Wilderness, after making a turn eastward we started driving the Glade Top Trail National Scenic Byway. Another set of roadside panoramic views presented themselves to us, as we drove along ridge tops and through the glades that surrounded them.

Find This Mill

On northbound Missouri Hwy 95 at Longrun, Missouri, go about four miles north on 95. Turn east on County Road D. Follow D generally southeast and turn left on south County Road 855 to where it joins County Road 848 and then a quarter mile to Hammond.

lat 36.676575° N lon 92.647077° W

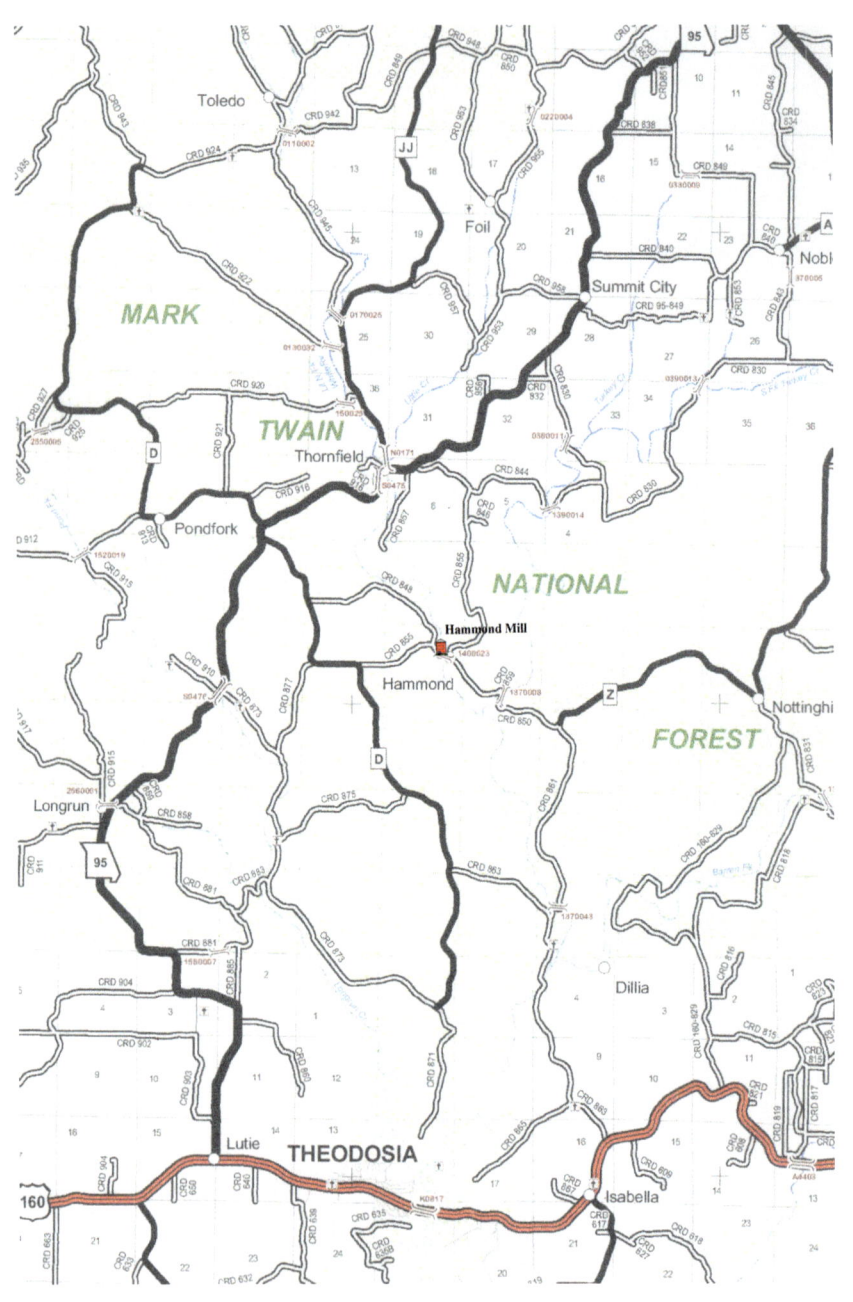

21

EDWARDS MILL
TANEY COUNTY

Edwards Mill is more than likely the only mill of its kind in the world. Built on the campus of College of the Ozarks, at Point Lookout, Missouri, the mill grinds cornmeal and grits (which you may purchase in the gift shop onsite), and also serves as a showcase for the various goods and art that students create while studying at this school.

In fact, there is a weaving studio upstairs in the mill, and many of the lovely products stand on display for sale. When I was onsite, I snapped a photo of two students working on baskets for sale. When they're not helping customers, they keep busy weaving.

For those of you not familiar with the concept of education at the College of the Ozarks, its mission statement reads, "The mission of College of the Ozarks is to provide the advantages of a Christian education for youth of both sexes, especially those found worthy, but who are without sufficient means to procure such training." The college offers a wide variety of majors, from nursing to business and accounting. Full-time students are required to participate in the Work Education Program, which also includes a wide variety of opportunities. As a result of this policy, the college has been dubbed "Hard Work U."

According to *From the Ozarks Oven: Edwards Mill Cookbook* (Betty Watts, College of the Ozarks, 1989), this mill "began as a poor man's dream." Mr. and Mrs. Hubert Edward, from Kansas City, financed an operational replica of an Ozarks grist mill in 1972, as imagined by William Cameron.

Cameron arrived in the U.S. from Ireland in 1923, and worked as a miller and as a mill product representative throughout the Ozarks for almost 50 years. It is reported that Cameron called upon 180 mills throughout his career, and he said, "Some of them as small as 25 barrels a day and others as large as 3,500 barrels." After World War II, Cameron opened his own feed mill in Exeter, Missouri.

The college called upon Cameron to lead the mill build. In order to create this historically accurate mill, Cameron had to find timber and equipment from older Missouri and Kansas mills, putting the various components all together to make a two-story mill with a 12-foot waterwheel. The website *State of the Ozarks* writes, "Authenticity is the theme of the mill. Massive timbers that form the framework were mortised and pegged in the tradition of pioneer structure, when iron fasteners were rare. The mill is made of native woods such as oak, maple and cedar."

At the time of the construction, Mr. Edward chaired the board of the Dixie-Portland Flour Mills, a Kansas City business. The College of the Ozarks dedicated Edwards Mill on October 7, 1972. Obviously, the mill is named for him.

Down in the Basement of Edwards Mill

The basement holds a museum, plumb full of artifacts about mills and the process involved. It even holds the equipment that the mill uses for grinding corn.

Outside Edwards Mill

Walk around the mill and you'll see more interesting items, such as mill stones from around the Ozarks on one side, and an elevated flume that brings water from the mill pond to the overshot wheel. The mill pond is fed by Lake Honor. I highly recommend walking around the building, to admire the rock work that features an arrow, along with the construction of the waterwheel and raceway. It's a work of art.

Find This Mill

The mill is located on the School of the Ozarks campus at One Opportunity Avenue, College of the Ozarks, Point Lookout, Mo. 65726. The gift shop also offers online shopping, where you may purchase any of the more than 30 items made by the students. Edwards Mill is open weekdays and Saturdays from 9 a.m. to 5 p.m. Closed on Sundays and holidays.

lat 36.617236° N lon 93.237475° W

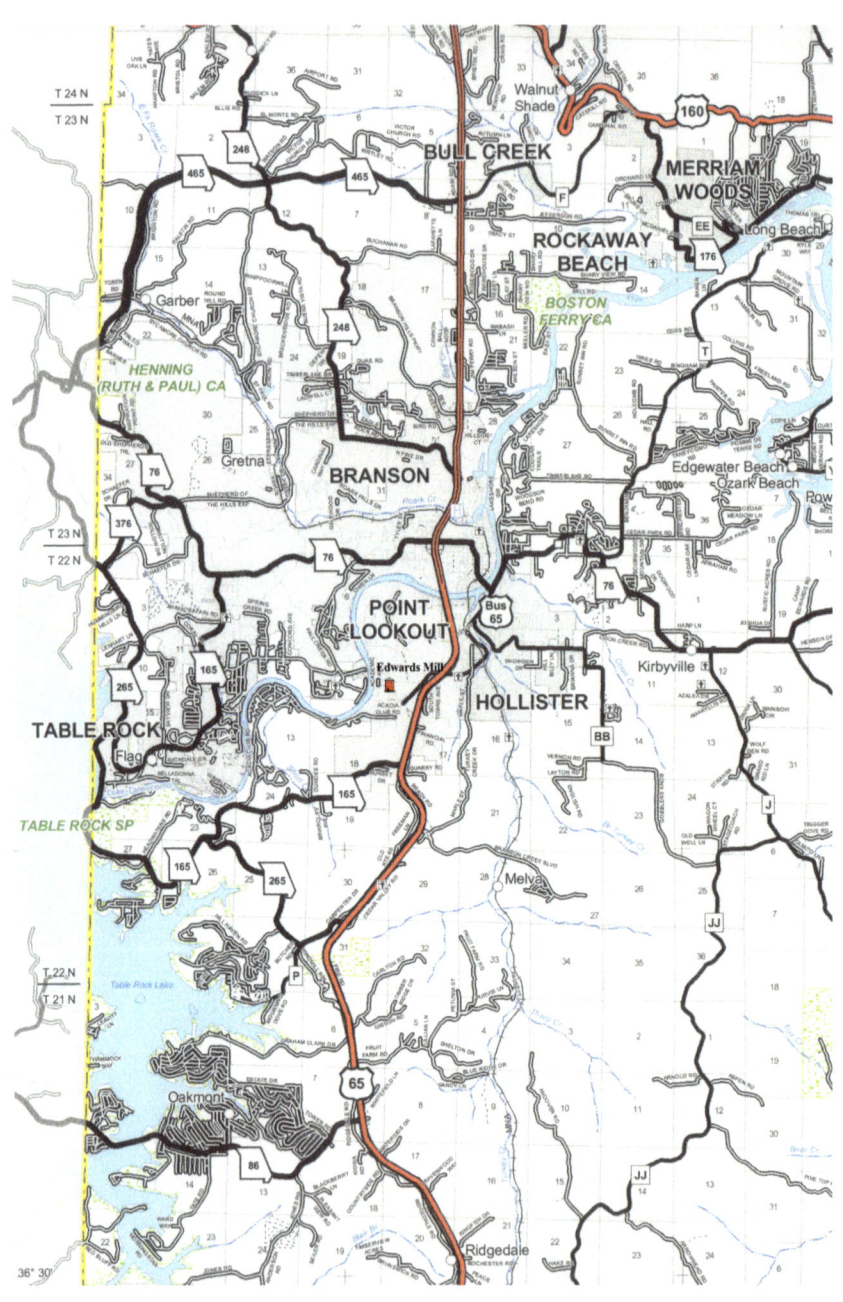

22

OZARK MILL

CHRISTIAN COUNTY

Sitting at the junction of the Finley River and the Ozark Trace (the area's mail delivery route), in Ozark, Missouri, stands the impressive (and some might say, imposing) Ozark Mill. On a beautiful autumn day, we visited the mill – courtesy of an invitation from Finley Farms. I had driven by the setting of the mill several times, and knew it was "in the works," but didn't expect it to be this grand and frankly, rustically beautiful.

According to *River of Farm Life* website, factors including accessibility and ability to dam a water source came into consideration for siting of this mill. As mentioned above, the location sat on an important mail route, as well. You'll see that feature tied to many a mill in the Ozarks. This mill also served as the community's post office. In fact, down the road from this mill, at Rockbridge Mill, you can see the edifice of its old post office. The Ozark Mill – formerly named the Kimberling Mill because of the family name associated with it – dates back to the early 1800s, and suffered (typical for mills in the 1800s) at least three major fires.

During the Civil War, many of the Ozarks' mills burned for various reasons. Not this one. The Confederates claimed the Ozark Mill and operated the mill during the war. Afterward, the mill helped this area of the country to rebuild efficiently, because it stood up and running and ready for action.

According to the history of the Ozark Mill, found at Finley Farms' website, in 1922 the second fire destroyed the mill. John Hawkins purchased the mill that year and began construction of a concrete dam that you can see today, to harness power from the river. The present mill building hearkens back to 1939. The Ozark Mill carries the distinction of being the last grist water mill to operate, and closed in 1992.

In 1993, Bass Pro Shop's Johnny Morris purchased the property, which includes Finley Farms. Perhaps one of the most dramatic and significant efforts to preserve the mill occurred in 2018, when a crew shifted the entire mill building, about 400 tons' worth, back 80 feet from the bank of the river so that the foundation could be restored. After being returned to its original setting, the mill site received new floodgates to control the power of the river.

What To Do in the Area

Today's setting at Finley Farms includes the historic Riverside Bridge, The Ozark Mill Restaurant, The Workshop (facility for local artisans, crafters and chefs to showcase and teach their talents in a coffee-shop setting), a Farmers Market, Market Shed, event spaces (such as The Garrison, The Riverside Room and The Hawkins Room) and an outdoor chapel for weddings and other events. Across the street, catty-corner from the mill sits the Hawkins' family's home, which is now a place where brides may organize and prepare for the big moment over across the bridge and in the chapel. The overall plan for Finley Farms has been managed by Morris's daughter, Megan.

I have eaten at the restaurant, both times sitting outdoors to view the river and bridge. The food is delicious and fresh, from seasonal market findings. After a meal, take a tour through the old mill, where shadow figures dance on the walls. Then, spend a few minutes in the well-stocked gift shop that features regional artists and items.

Find This Mill

The Ozark Mill is located at 802 Finley Farms Lane, Ozark, Missouri.
lat 37.026853° N lon 93.207934° W

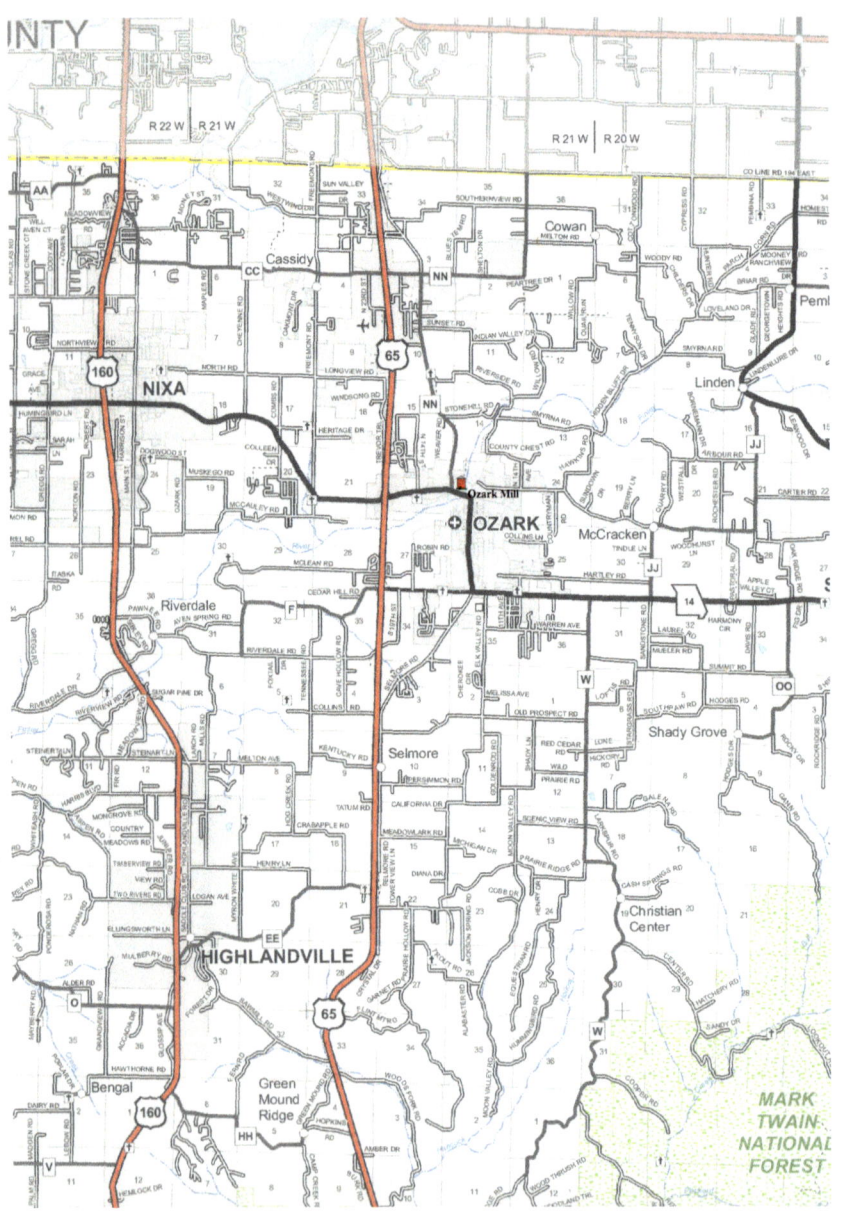

23

WOMMACK MILL
GREENE COUNTY

The Wommack Mill commands a second look from passersby. Sitting a short distance off the small town main street in a park setting, the mill is now like the central nervous system of the town of Fair Grove. In fact, the first time I visited Fair Grove, I felt compelled to park nearby, get out of my car and walk over to the big, beautiful wooden building.

Later, I would meet Mary Terry, board president of the Fair Grove Historical and Preservation Society, for a guided tour of this mill – one of only three operating steam-powered mills left in the United States.

Mary Terry, board president of the Fair Grove Historical and Preservation Society, stands beside the steam engine flywheel in the engine room of the Wommack Mill.

Mary said, "When you go through Fair Grove, it really hasn't changed much, except for what's in the buildings now." She ought to know, since she's lived here since she was 9 and her husband has been here all his life.

About the mills she added, "A lot of people ask, 'Where's the water wheel?' Well, we've never ever had one. The creek out here never flowed all the time. You can see where it was dammed up and water carried in." The mill was run with steam power from a single cylinder steam engine, then electricity, followed by gasoline and diesel engines.

Built in 1883, the original mill measured 30-feet by 40-feet and stood 40-feet tall. It was named after its owners, and called the Boegel and Hine Flour Mill. (Boegel is pronounced beagle.) Mary showed me a document created for tours by Dan Manning, who has been instrumental in the restoration process of the mill, and it listed 20 owners (a mix of people and organizations) throughout the years. Ethel and Clifford Wommack owned it from 1943 until Clifford died in 1969. It was sold in 1970.

Dan writes that in 1900 three roller mills were added. A ledger on display from December 1920 displays these numbers: 52,200 pounds of patent flour, 6,750 pounds of shorts (mixture of bran, grain and coarse meal), 14,750 pounds of bran (outside layer of a kernel of wheat), 13,585 pounds of corn meal and 7,100 pounds of chops (coarsely ground grain). By 1927, the mill had switched to making only animal feed for cattle, hogs, sheep and poultry. Mary speculated that because of transportation improvements, and the availability of bread and other wheat/corn products in grocery stores, people didn't have to bring home-grown corn and wheat to the miller any longer.

Mary pointed out the two 32-foot tall, 17-foot in diameter concrete/creek gravel silos standing alongside the mill, built in 1917. Poorly designed, these silos failed to keep wheat fresh, and as result, it molded and had to be used for hog feed. Since then, the fine folk of Fair Grove like to use the twin silos as backdrops for all types of photograph sessions. With ivy creeping upward, and the old mill alongside, the pair makes an interesting setting.

The Fair Grove Historical and Preservation Society purchased the mill and some acreage in 1984 for $6,000. Dan and his wife, Betty, had moved to Fair Grove from California in 1974 – an "escape to the country" of sorts. They became acquainted with local resident Jerry Thomas. Before they took on the restoration process involved with the mill, the Mannings and Jerry – along with other community people – began working on an old cemetery. In 1977, the Historical and Preservation Society was founded.

Mary said, "Jerry was a local, and generations of his family lived in this area. He saw a vision of this mill and wanted to save it." By 1986, the National Historic Register of Historic Places added the Boegel and Hine Flour Mill to its list.

Throughout the years, the Society has undertaken major reconstruction projects. Here are a few, including lifting the building to add a new foundation. Reconstruction of the engine room brought in cut limestone rocks from a dairy barn near the mill. Four-pane, double-hung sash windows came from an old schoolhouse south of Springfield.

A single-cylinder, 30-horsepower, stationary steam engine – originally manufactured in 1900 and purchased by the Society from an Oklahoma sawmill – had to be completely restored. The second floor's oak floor became the first floor's flooring, because the original floor was gone. The Society added a front porch, which now hosts weddings, family reunions and other events. A Cowboy Church holds services on Sundays inside the mill.

Members of the Society have scoured auctions and sales to find roller mills, a vertical steam engine, a feed mill, corn sheller and the list goes on. A walk through the main floor of the museum is testament to the sweat equity of these volunteers. The walls are filled with photographs, in chronological order, detailing the mill's history and its significance to the town.

A collection of well-worn overalls adorns a back wall. "You see those old overalls?" asked Mary. "I can see those men in them, because I knew them."

Original to the mill, two 42-inch buhrstones made their way from a quarry in France to Indianapolis, where they were "dressed," cemented and bound together. The top stone weighs 1,400 pounds.

In the basement, in addition to the steam engines, boiler and pulley system for the mill, collections of horse harnesses, tools and equipment serve as further museum pieces and essential gear. It's an eclectic combination, well-tended.

Mary added, "This mill functions; you get to see it grind during the festival. During the ice cream social, which we just had July 20, we run the boiler and the steam engine, so you have a sense of that sound and smell and just all those cool things."

In that last quote, she references two ongoing annual events, both started by the Society in the '70s: the ice cream social (third weekend in July) and the festival – the Fair Grove Heritage Reunion – which is held on the last full weekend in September.

Looking toward the future concerns Mary greatly. She said, "We're a very small group – very, very small group. I can't get interest from the younger generation and I keep telling them, 'This will go away.' ... Dan tells me, 'Mary, we've been fortunate, and people will step in.'"

In the tour notes, Dan optimistically concludes, "This mill continues to serve the Fair Grove community as a social meeting center, like it has done since 1883."

What To Do in the Area

A tour of the Wommack Mill can be arranged by calling 417-759-2807. You may also want to see the nearby Historical Society Museum, walk the grounds and check out the cabins constructed by the Society. Then, hop back in the car and drive up the main street to the historical cemetery, which holds not only human remains, but also, two local, trusty mules, Jack and Pete, purchased from Oda Shipman by the Mannings. The illustrious pair appeared at parades and other celebratory events in the area back in the day.

Visit the Fair Grove Historical and Preservation Society website.

Find This Mill

Located about 10 miles north of I-44 in Springfield, the Wommack Mill is on the corner of Old Mill Road (Route 125) and Main Street.

lat 37.383060° N, long 93.150476° W

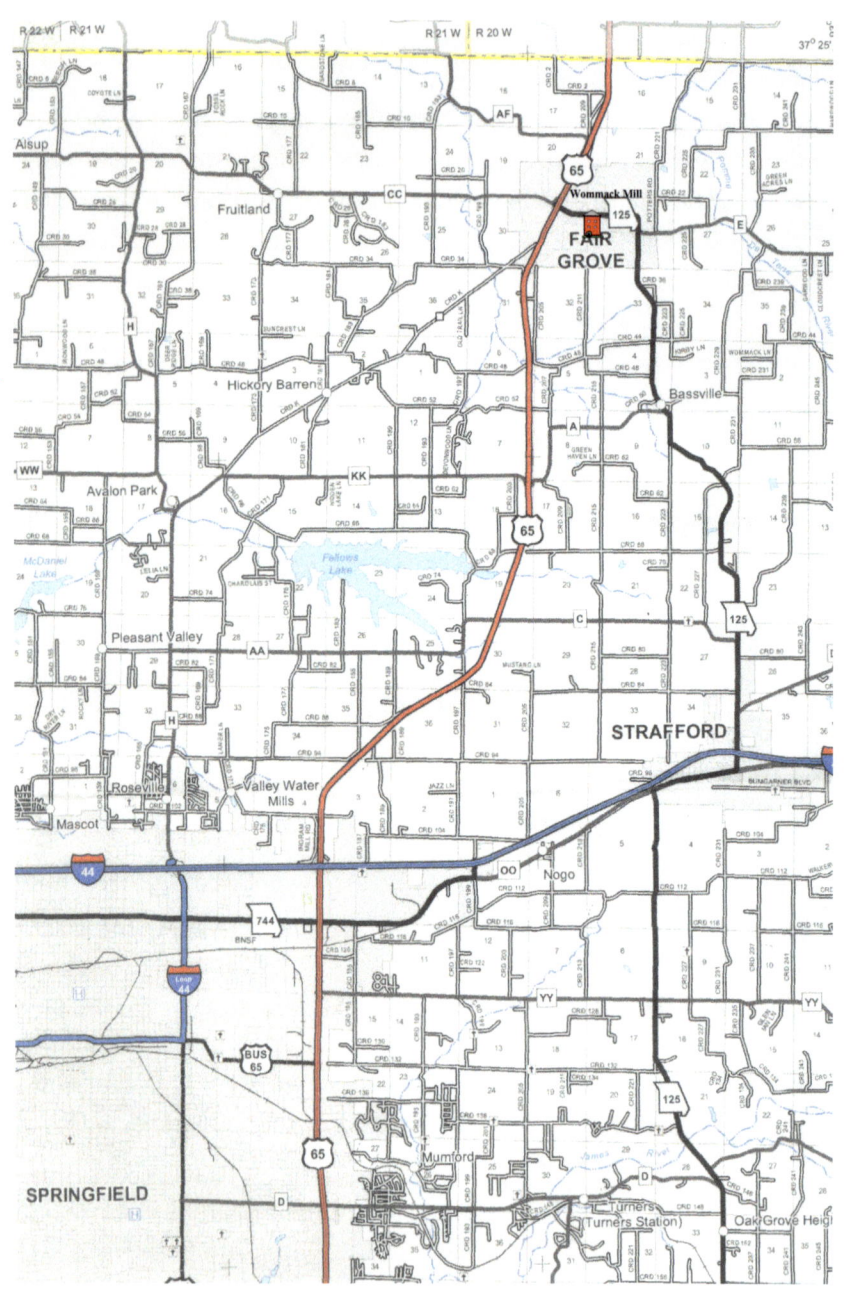

24

HULSTON MILL
DADE COUNTY

Hulston Mill belongs in an elite and small group of two existing water mills in the Missouri Ozarks (that I can think of, anyway) that can claim having been moved from streamside to another setting. Right off the top of my head, the other mill is the Ozark Mill, found at Finley Farms in Ozark, Missouri.

Dade County used to have 10 mills, and Hulston is the last one of the lot still equipped to demonstrate how a mill operated. Built in 1840 at the confluence of the Sac River and Turnback Creek, the mill ground flour and corn. According to the Dade County Historical Society, at *State of the Ozarks'* website, Ezekiel Madison Campbell constructed the original mill.

That mill washed away, so Campbell built a new mill farther up the Sac River. As is the history of gristmills, several owners and millers worked onsite throughout the years. As is also the case of mills from this era, the Civil War dealt a blow to many gristmills; especially, if the mills couldn't be of service to the cause. It's not unusual to read that in the 1860s, mills were burned. This one, however, played a significant role in sending flour to units of the Union Army that occupied Springfield, Missouri, in 1861, so it survived.

Henry Engleman purchased the mill in 1859. Supposedly, Engleman – being from Virginia and a Southern sympathizer – was not keen to sell his grain to the Union, and specifically, to Gen. Nathaniel Lyon's soldiers. In a well-made documentary by *Ozarks-Watch Video Magazine,* from 2019, Dale Moore talks to Kent Parrish, of the Dade County Historical Society. Parrish said the Dade County Mounted Volunteers, led by Clark Wright (who went on to be a Colonel in the 6th Missouri Cavalry at the battle of Vicksburg) were tasked to get supplies for Lyon in Dade County.

The Historical Society also opined that without the flour from this and other mills in Dade County, the Union troops would not have been able to fight and win the battle at Wilson's Creek in August 1861. The Army would have been forced to find sustenance farther north, and the battle might have been delayed until a later date.

After the Civil War, the mill's namesake, James Christopher Hulston, purchased the mill in 1875. A village with a livery stable, blacksmith shop, post office, general store, drug store and later, a tomato cannery sprung up around the mill. In 1892, Hulston's grandson, John Christopher Hulston, modernized the mill, and at this point it became a full roller mill equipped with an auxiliary steam engine to provide a back-up system to the stream-powered turbine in drought conditions.

Parrish said that John even marketed his own flour, known as Hulston Gilt flour.

Hulston was murdered in 1897, and his family sold the mill in 1912 to the Nixons, who then sold it two years later. This pattern continued on and on (without murder) – at least five more millers operated this mill for a total span of 127 years. Parrish said he believes the mill ran for reasons of commerce until the 1940s. After that, it was a hobby. On June 25, 1967, Hulston Mill performed its last commercial grind. Also, at this time construction of Stockton Lake made flooding of the mill an imminent prospect.

Through the fund-raising and other efforts of local people, the Dade County Historical Society, the park board and the county court, the mill was moved from its place on the river to a nearby (1.5 miles away) 50-acre parcel of land, now known as the Hulston Mill Historical Park.

The site officially opened in 1969 and became a magnet, a focal point, for the heritage-affiliated park. It should be noted that this project was the first project of the Historical Society. Parrish said they had hoped that someday the state would be interested in taking on the preservation and maintenance, but that it hadn't happened (and still hasn't, apparently).

The park holds the mill, along with the Weir cabin that was built in the 1800s. The Weir cabin's summer kitchen sits behind the house.

When we visited the park on a warm day in February, we enjoyed sitting at a picnic table near the mill and conjuring what it must have been like in its heyday. Unfortunately pigeons had access to the mill building via holes in the roofline and other openings in the building walls, which can't be good for the structure. One of the cabins onsite had suffered a collapsed ceiling, and it looked like renovations in the Wier cabin had been abandoned.

Parrish mentioned that the Hulston Family Foundation had been involved somehow with the mill at one time.

Unfortunately, it looks as though the yearly Civil War reenactments are a thing of the past here. Some groups, such as trail riders and primitive skill enthusiasts, still hold events. It appears the only way to contact anyone from the Dade County Historical Society is on its Facebook page or on the Huston Mill Facebook page.

What to Do in the Area

Hulston Mill has the trailhead for a 14-mile multi-use hike / bike / horse trail that winds over to Stockton Lake. It also serves as a site for several organizational gatherings, featuring trail rides and festivals. Primitive and electric campsites are available, first come-first serve.

Find This Mill

The mill's address is 6 Hulston Mill Lane, Everton, Missouri. In Dade County, take Hwy 160 to Hwy EE. Turn north, following Hwy EE to a gravel road called Hulston Mill Park Road on your right. Turn right and follow to the parking lot/camping area on the right.

lat 37.441197° N lon 93.713036° W

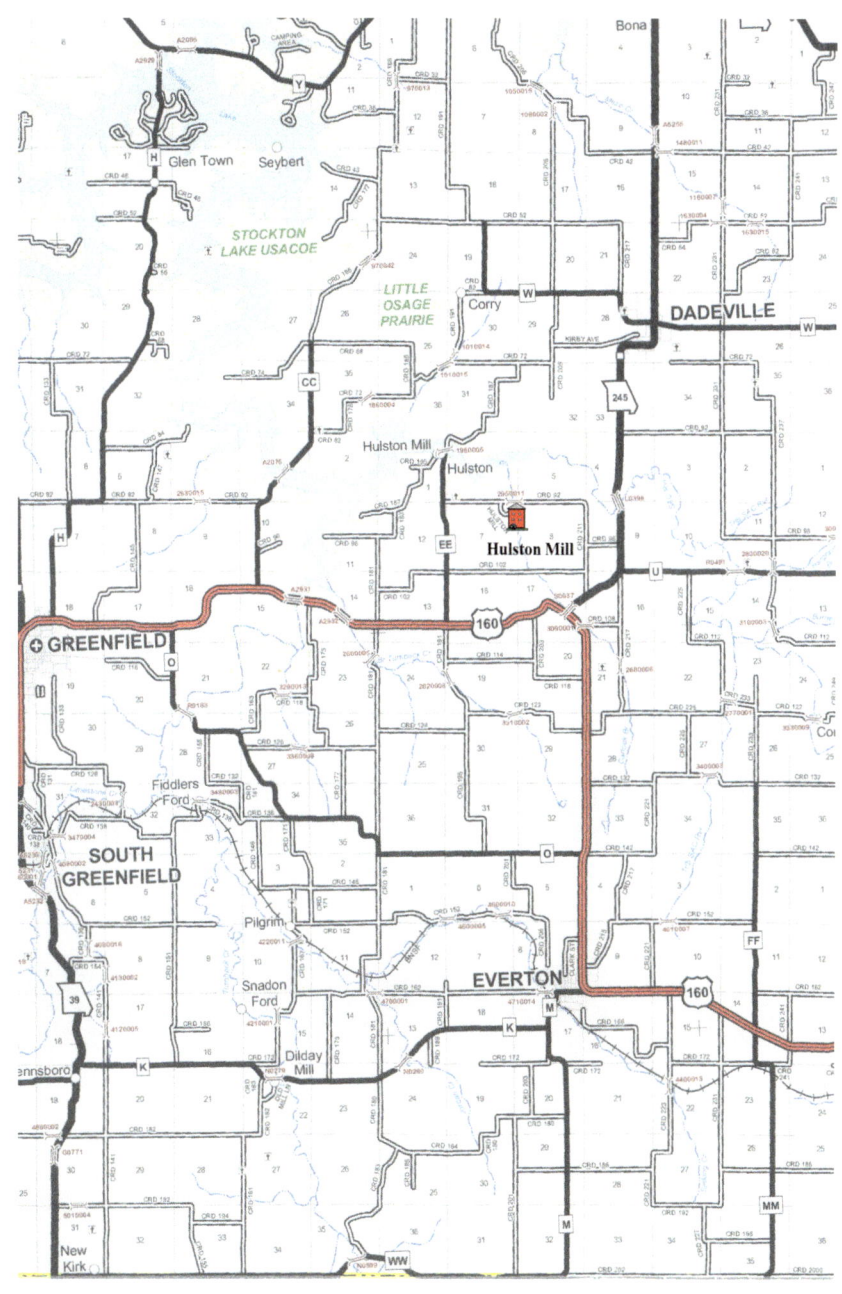

25

BRITAIN MILL
DADE COUNTY

I have longed to visit Britain Mill since I first discovered it online
before Covid hit. Isn't it interesting? We are now dating things in our
lives pre- and post-Covid. I finally got an opportunity to arrange for a
visit and headed to Ash Grove, Missouri, in Feburary 2024, after
contacting mill owners Clyde and Janet Beal, who have lovingly
restored the mill.

Clyde and Janet Beal, inside the mill in 2024

When I use the term "lovingly," I mean it, for the Beals fell in love with the old mill upon seeing it advertised for sale in a country magazine back in the early 2000s. Janet said that the minute she saw the advertisement for the mill and artist's cottage, she felt that it was calling to them. The place intrigued both of them, so they quickly came up from Florida to Missouri to see it. They purchased the tract of land that included a mill and outbuildings, along with a small house that had belonged to an artist. Clyde majored in Physics and worked as director of operations for Lockheed-Martin, and he came equipped with basic knowledge of the mechanics, which he applied to operating a mill, and learning more about how a mill works. Janet has been his "right-hand woman" throughout the years.

Then, the work began. Not only have they rolled up their sleeves to restore and maintain this property over the intervening years, but also, they decided to invite the public (by appointment only) to see it.

Clyde compiled the mill's history thoroughly in a post at the Britain Mill website. If you're interested in this mill's history, please read his account.

History of Britain Mill

To summarize the mill's history, it is thought to have been constructed sometime between 1839 and 1845. The mill began as Turnback Mill, since it sat on Turnback Creek, and had its name changed several times. The last owners of a viable mill were named ... Britain.

Britain Mill was not burned during the Civil War, as many mills in southwestern Missouri were. Clyde writes, "In fact, the First Kansas Volunteers camped at what is now Paris Springs, half a mile downstream from the mill, for a few days in July, 1861. One soldier's letter survives, recounting an encounter with a Rebel cavalry patrol and the Union pickets. The same soldier mentions that the mill '...is at work night and day...' providing the troops with much needed flour." It's thought that since the mill owners were Quaker and Union sympathizers, their mill was spared the fate of many other mills in southern Missouri, which were burned by Union troops.

Turnback Creek begins its journey near Billings, Missouri, and winds its way northward 30 miles before it gets to Britain Mill. Turnback ends at Stockton Lake. Goose Creek flows nearby and it joins Turnback just upstream of the mill.

In 1892, the family who owned the mill, the Likins, added a Leffels water turbine and a second story to the building, which housed new equipment including a Great Western roller. This meant the water wheel would no longer be needed. There is a 4- to 5-foot (in diameter) wheel box onsite that would have accommodated either a paddle or a water wheel. Clyde believes the wheel box is circa 1857.

The last name, Britain, came from the family who ran the mill operation the longest. Interestingly, their daughter, Bette, began to operate the mill as a miller – typically a man's job – sometime before the 1940s.

Generally, Missouri's water mills began a descent into ruin and abandonment about this time because electric (and sometimes steam) power allowed for larger industrial and more efficient operations. The availability of better means of transportation than horse- or mule-drawn wagons, along with better roads, also signaled an end to the requirement for milling operations and their associated services to be close by farmers' properties.

Sometime after World War II, Britain Mill underwent a major restoration, representing the love people have for historic water mills, why the Beals bought this water mill and why I have written this book about mills in the Missouri Ozarks.

Bill Cameron, a notable expert on water mill construction, managed the Britain Mill restoration. He also is responsible for the beautiful design and construction of Edwards Mill, located on the campus of College of the Ozarks, near Point Lookout, Missouri. Bill's wife, Letha, had spent time at the Britain Mill with the family and recalled those days as some of her "fondest."

Today's little red mill doesn't stand where the original mill stood, but is only a stone's throw away. You can still see two sluices and the old mill race and turbine pit in the ground nearby. You can see Turnback Creek, too.

We were so fortunate that Clyde walked with us to see pieces of the restored dam on Turnback. In 1988, after artist Vivian Boswell bought the property, she obtained the proper approval (Corps of Engineers and others) to construct a new spillway. Just four months later, a "500-year-flood" destroyed the new construction. There are a few parts and pieces left from the project, at the edges.

After the Beals bought the property in 2002, they began to think of restoring it. In 2004, they hired project manager Harold Sullins, who worked at Montauk State Park, east of Licking, Missouri, which also has an old mill onsite.

The property had suffered from the terrible flooding, and none of the equipment or gear had been cleaned since a flood in 1993. Clyde writes, "The project goal was to restore the operations sufficiently to demonstrate to selected visitors how a custom mill might operate in the mid-19th century in the Ozarks. Initially, the existing equipment was cleaned and restored. The bran duster was fitted with screens for corn meal and grits to serve as a sifter, eventually. The restoration of water power was deferred for a later time, so plans for electrically powered equipment were made."

And, of course, there were more projects in the works for the Beals ... Clyde and Janet told tales of slogging away for more than 72 hours after a recent flooding a few years ago, to haul mud from the basement of the mill building – in buckets handed up and dumped out. They said it was back-breaking work.

Clyde offered to show us more of the 50-acre property, which has a walking trail with 27 cairns.

He is like a mountain goat, with his sneakers on, winding his way uphill through scrabble and showing us the improvements he has made throughout the years to his beloved property.

He and Janet may be in the sunset years of their lives, and they may not be able to dig out mud from flooding anymore, but they can look upon their mill with pride and satisfaction that for this generation, they have made a difference.

When asked why he decided to spend his retirement years restoring this old mill, Clyde summed it up: "I feel the need to be productive."

Please visit the Beals' website for more information. Open by appointment only.

Find This Mill

You can see Britain Mill from the road. The address is 5922 Lawrence 1207, Ash Grove, Missouri, which is about 20 miles southwest of Springfield, Missouri.

lat 37.189255° N lon 93.685375° W

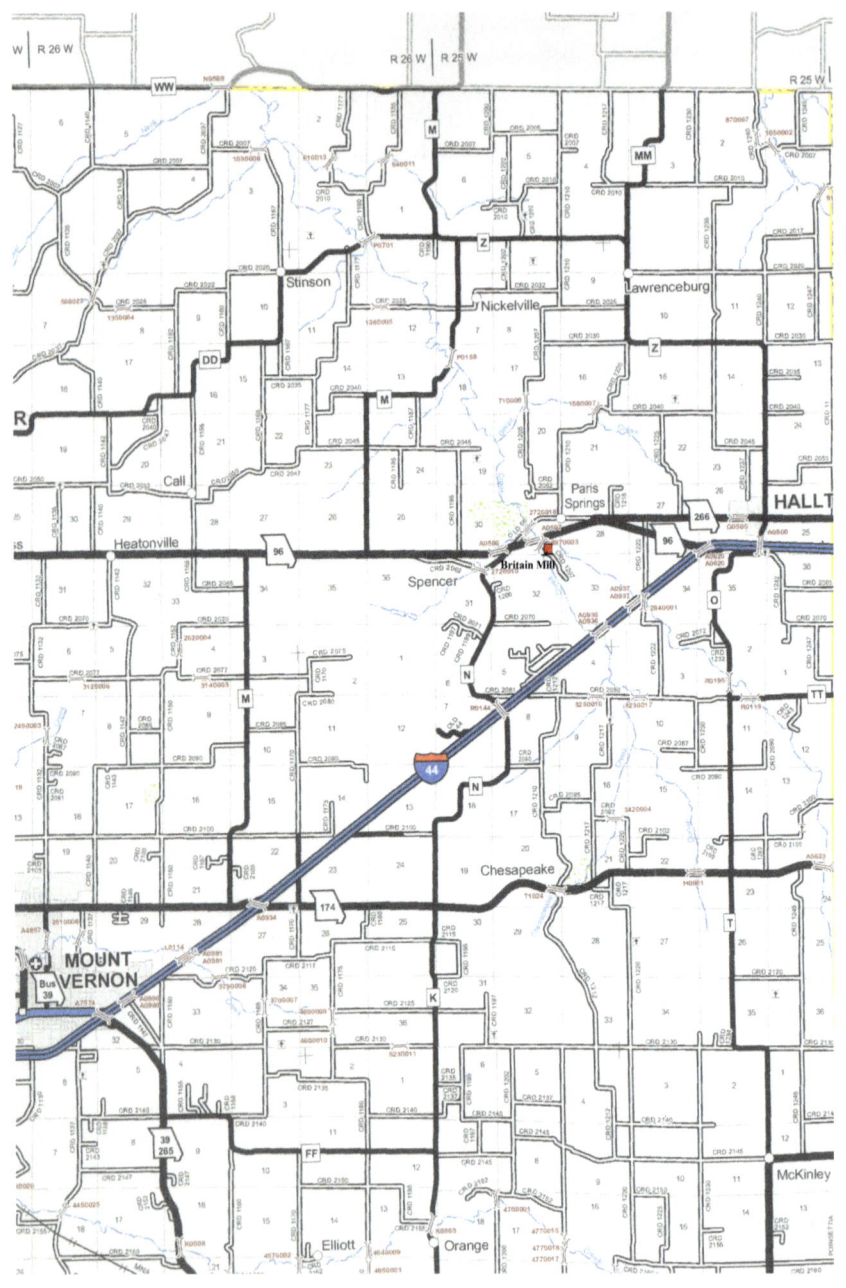

26

JOLLY MILL
NEWTON COUNTY

Not a breath of fresh air moved on that day. In sweltering heat, we spent more than an hour wandering around Jolly Mill Park, located about four miles southeast of Pierce City, Missouri. The park has been developed around the mill, a unique way of honoring a past culture and presence that had been pivotal at one time for the success of this area. I barely noticed the heat and humidity because this is a place I have wanted to see for a long time. If you know me, you'll know that I go a-gaga over old mills and springs. This one did not disappoint.

Slaves built the mill in 1837 for Thomas Isbell and his son, John. Originally, the family named it the Isbell Mill. Sitting on Capps Creek, not only did the mill grind grain with its fancy French buhr-stones, but it also distilled whiskey. In fact, it began as a distillery. The structure – three stories of pit-sawed boards attached to hand-hewn logs and held together with handmade wooden pegs – appears to have withstood the test of time (thanks to the efforts of concerned local citizens). The huge mill stands on a foundation made of hand-cut limestone slabs, sans mortar, that according to George G. Suggs, Jr., in *Water Mills of the Missouri Ozarks*, came from a quarry nearby in Barry County.

The mill, as mills did back then, served as a social gathering place for people who brought their grain to be ground. It also catered to the stagecoach and wagon train crowds. Isbell decided he didn't want to pay taxes on whiskey sometime in the 1870s, and the mill focused its attentions on grain. Isbell also added general stores and a blacksmith shop. With a major road passing the site from Springfield, the mill benefitted from that convenience, as well as the demand for its grinding services.

Civil War Story

It's not uncommon to hear about mills being burnt to the ground during the Civil War, especially in southwest Missouri where skir-mishes abounded and the Bald Knobbers ran amuck. During the Civil War, Suggs writes that Isbell "vanished" from the area – at that time, a village called Jollification. The mill stood silent. Even though a skirmish ensued in Jollification and down in nearby Ritchey, the mill stood unscathed. Then, George Isbell purchased the mill, writes Scuggs, at a sheriff's sale.

Enter the Frisco Railroad, which laid tracks too far from the mill for any advantage of the business. By the mid-1870s, Jollification had been reduced to Jolly, and George Isbell – who had once again started the business of whiskey distilling, along with grain grinding – gave up the distillery side of the business. George Isbell enlarged the mill and in 1894, sold it to George I. Brown, his nephew. Brown, according to Suggs, further enlarged the mill and brought in an underwater turbine to use instead of the standard undershot wheel. By this time, the mill became known as Jolly Mill.

History is sketchy about the mill until about 1912, when it's reported (again by Suggs) that A.C. Lucas and Son owned the mill, Jolly Rolling Mills. W. F. Haskins then purchased it and added a second turbine. Suggs says that production declined after WWI, and ended in 1973.

Jolly Mill Park Foundation

Local citizens created the Jolly Mill Park Foundation in 1983, for the purpose of restoring the old mill and to add a local recreation area. They saw success, and the mill was listed on the National Register of Historic Places. Picnic areas and fishing opportunities are abundant. On the day I visited, a mom and her two kids walked up to the parking lot from fishing downstream. The Missouri Department of Conservation stocks four miles of the associated stream at this location with rainbow and brown trout. It's considered a "White Ribbon Trout Area."

Everything seemed to be running well after the restoration, with grist mill demonstrations onsite ... until the flood of December 2015, which decimated the park's covered bridge and filled the mill full of mud. The next spring, the Foundation held its first Annual Jolly Mill Challenge, a fun run and 5k race. At least 227 runners showed up, and ponied up money to restore the bridge, parking lot, sidewalks and other features of the park.

Chapman School

The park also contains the Chapman School, aka Hazel Hill School. Built in 1884, this school claims the title of the first public school in Barry Country School District No. 1. It closed the doors to education in the spring of 1951. The J.H. Chapman family donated the school to the Jolly Mill Park Foundation in 1985. The Foundation moved the school from its site – 1.5 miles away – to the park and restored it. It sits next to a modern playground, an interesting juxtaposition between the old and the new.

What to Do in the Area

Capps Creek Conservation Area is located across from Jolly Mill. The MDC stocks brown and rainbow trout throughout the year in the area that flows from Jolly Mill Park to the confluence of Shoal Creek.

Find This Mill

Jolly Mill Park is located at 31630 Jolly Mill Drive, Pierce City, Missouri. It is about 50 miles southwest of Springfield.

lat 36.897271° N lon 94.071676° W

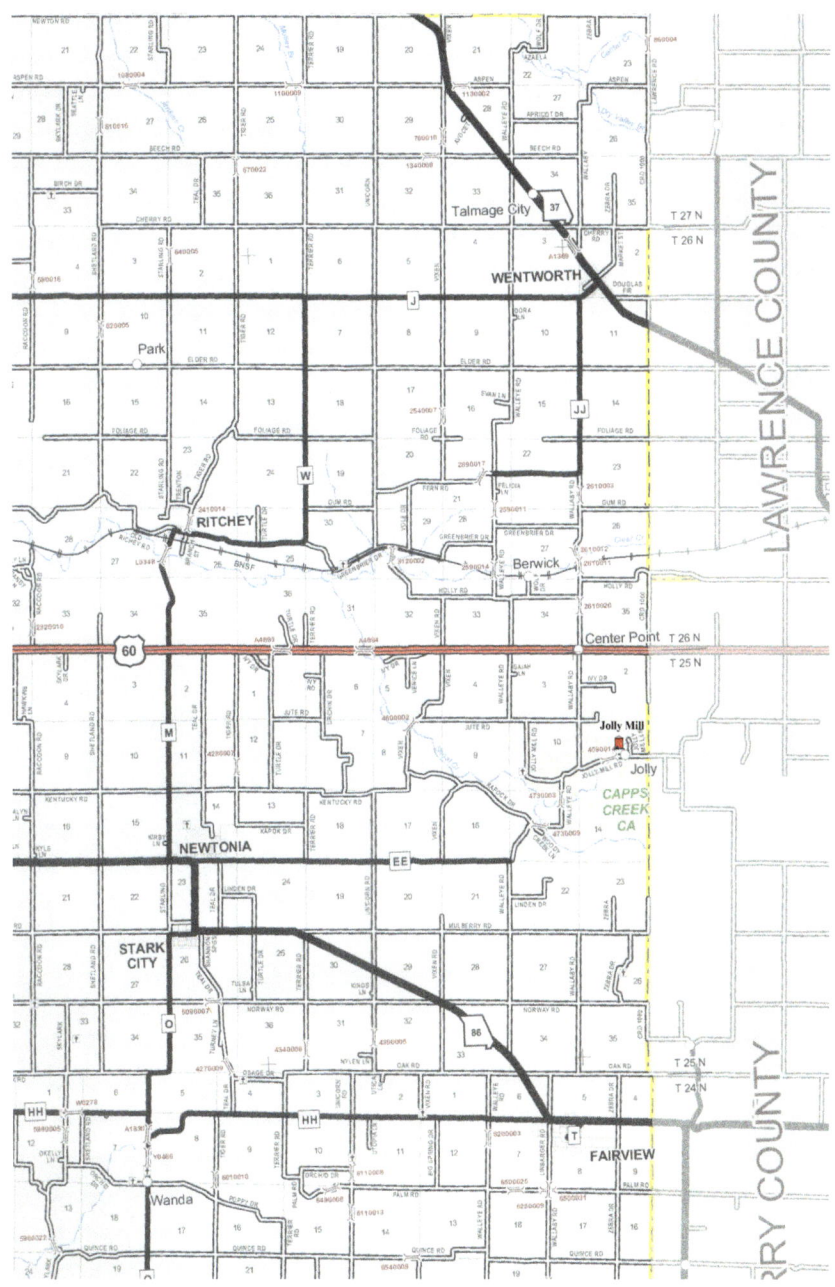

RESOURCES

A History of Ozark County, 1841-1991, on CD, Ozark County Historium, Gainesville, Missouri, 2023.

Historic Ozarks Mills, Mike McCarthy, 2009, Photoozarks, offered by Rural Missouri. This beautiful hard-bound book is filled with color photos of more than 25 mills in southern Missouri and northern Arkansas, with historical information and directions to all the mills.

A Living History of the Ozarks, Phyllis Rossiter, 1992, Pelican Publishing Company. Rossiter is another voice of the Ozarks, and this book is filled with mills, as well as other historical places.

Springs of Missouri, Gerald L. Vineyard, Missouri Geological Survey And Water Resources, 1982. A thorough compilation of Missouri's springs. May mention a mill occasionally as being associated with a spring.

Water Mills of the Missouri Ozarks, George G. Suggs, 1990, University of Oklahoma Press. Paintings and illustrations by Jake K. Wells. Written by two professors from Southeast Missouri University (Suggs and Wells), this book is lovely, vividly illustrated with watercolors by Wells, along with historical descriptions by Suggs, and vignettes of the mills.

ACKNOWLEDGMENTS

Thank you to all the tour guides, millers and people in Missouri dedicated to keeping history alive for new generations to enjoy. Also, thank you to the state of Missouri, for recognizing the importance of our state's milling heritage.

ABOUT THE AUTHOR

I was student teaching at Rolla High School, sophomore English, in 1999. Part of the curriculum included Anne Tyler's short stories. I liked her style of writing and read her books, including *The Accidental Tourist*. Meanwhile, back at the university, I had just finished three years of study in English with a professor, Dr. Larry Vonalt, who demanded that I write to the best of my ability. Sometimes, it would take five or six tries before he would accept a thesis for my research papers in the capstone course. He was like the curmudgeon professor in *The Paper Chase*. When I graduated from college in December 1999, there were no teaching positions available. So, I substitute taught, but couldn't get the notion of writing out of my head. How did other people do it for a living? How cool would that be, to be able to get paid for my words?

So, I started learning about freelance writing. One of my mentors, a woman in the local area, had written some articles that she sold to *Field and Stream*. I met her and she gave me great advice. I started sending queries to magazines.

Also, I called the editor of a nearby small town weekly newspaper office, the *St. James Leader-Journal*, and requested an appointment with him to discuss a new column idea I had, based on traveling in the Ozarks. I wanted to call it "The Accidental Ozarkian," and it was modeled after a character in Tyler's aforementioned book, a travel writer that takes people from their armchairs to places he described.

The editor agreed to run my column on a weekly basis, but told me, "I'm afraid you'll run out of things to write about in a year or two." The column ran for seven years and appeared in 10 publications, including newspapers and regional magazines, throughout the state. In 2002, Gov. Holden named me one of Missouri's "influential journalists" and I was invited to the Governor's Mansion for a reception.

I eventually worked as the managing editor of that newspaper, and honed my writing skills — covering local politics, school events, editing lunch menus and bowling scores, which also included having coffee with the locals at the diner in the mornings. I was invited to go divining in the local Catholic graveyard, as a result.

In 2006, I stopped writing the column to focus more attention on outdoor and travel magazines, creating the only publication online to feature women who shoot, hunt, fish and lead adventurous outdoor lives, *Women's Outdoor News*. In 2007, I received the award "Conservation Communicator of the Year" from the Conservation Federation of Missouri.

I now contribute occasional blog posts to my website, *The Accidental Ozarkian*, and will be compiling a few books that feature the collections of columns from years gone by. In my spare time, I will continue to go creekin' with my grandchildren, hunt, fish and enjoy our beautiful Ozarks with my family and friends.

What is The Accidental Ozarkian?

Presently, it is a travel blog with 80,266 readers and 2,194,312 pageviews in 2023. It features people and places in the Ozarks, as seen through my eyes, a woman from South Dakota – an enthusiastic transplant. The blog includes previously published works, including several mills, along with fresh content.

"The Accidental Ozarkian" has appeared throughout the years in these publications:

- *The St. James Leader Journal*
- *The Rolla Daily News*
- *The Waynesville Daily Guide*

- *The Mountain Grove News Journal*
- *The Sun Leader*
- *Cuba Free Press*
- *Outdoor Guide*
- *The Kaleidoscope Weekly*
- *Outdoor Journal*
- *Ozarks Mountaineer*

My bylines for other topics have appeared in the following magazines and newspapers:

- *Missouri Life*
- *Rural Missouri*
- *St. Louis Post Dispatch*
- *Kansas City Magazine*
- *AAA: Southern Traveler*
- *AAA: Midwest Traveler*
- *Show Me Missouri*
- *Springfield News Leader*
- *University of Missouri Alumni News Magazine*
- *Heartland USA*
- *Turkey Country*
- *American Hunter*
- *American Rifleman*
- *Fly Fisherman Magazine*
- *America's First Freedom*
- *Kansas Magazine*
- *Field and Stream*
- *Outdoor Life*

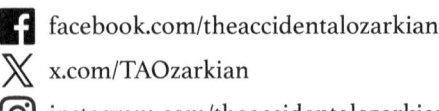

facebook.com/theaccidentalozarkian

x.com/TAOzarkian

instagram.com/theaccidentalozarkian

www.ingramcontent.com/pod-product-compliance
Lightning Source LLC
Chambersburg PA
CBHW040855120626
46551CB00001B/23